The POWER Series

DESERT SHIELD

The Build-Up: The Complete Story

Robert F. Dorr

Motorbooks International
Publishers & Wholesalers ®

First published in 1991 by Motorbooks International Publishers & Wholesalers, P O Box 2, 729 Prospect Avenue, Osceola, WI 54020 USA

Library of Congress Cataloging-in-Publication Data
Dorr, Robert F.
    Desert Shield / Robert F. Dorr.
      p.   cm.
    ISBN 0-87938-506-5
    1. Operation Desert Shield, 1990-   2. Iraq-Kuwait Crisis, 1990-   3. United States—Armed Forces—Saudi Arabia. I. Title. II. Series.
    DS79.72.D67   1991   90-24578
    956.704'3—dc20

On the front cover: An HMMWV gunner wears Bedouin-style protection against the harsh environment in Saudi Arabia. *DoD*

On the back cover: An HMMWV, or "Humm-Vee," sets out on patrol in the Saudi desert. *DoD* **Lower inset:** A Marine in full nuclear, biological and chemical (NBC) warfare suit guards the perimeter outside the 3rd Battalion, 9th Marines' base camp. *DoD* **Upper inset:** An F-14 launches off the deck of the USS *Independence*. On October 1, 1990, the *Independence* entered the Persian Gulf—the first carrier to operate in the gulf's narrow waters in seventeen years. *US Navy*

On the title page: American soldiers arrived in the deserts of the Middle East stocked with weaponry and plenty of water. These troopers belong to the 1st Cavalry Division. They are seen on arrival at an airbase in Saudi Arabia on October 12, 1990. *Robert F. Dorr*

On the frontispiece: Cool, clear water. Operation Desert Shield rewrote all the textbooks about how much water the human body needs or should take in. Army and Marine troops on the ground in Saudi Arabia were instructed to consume up to 5 gallons (19 liters) of the stuff in a 24 hour period. *US Army*

Printed and bound in the United States of America

In Memorium

August 1 to October 15, 1990

Major John M. Gordon, Major Richard W. Chase, Master Sergeant Rosendo Herrera, Technical Sergeant Daniel G. Perez, Major Richard M. Price, Staff Sergeant Edward E. Sheffield and Senior Master Sergeant Carpio Villarreal, Jr., of the 68th Military Airlift Squadron, 433rd Military Airlift Wing.

Staff Sergeant Daniel Garza and Staff Sergeant Lonty A. Knutson of the 433rd Organizational Maintenance Squadron, 433rd Military Airlift Wing.

Staff Sergeant John Campisi of the 55th Organizational Maintenance Squadron, 55th Strategic Reconnaissance Wing.

Major Peter S. Hook and Captain James B. Poulet of the 336th Tactical Fighter Squadron, 4th Tactical Fighter Wing.

Major Barry K. Henderson and Major Stephen G. Schramm of the 117th Tactical Reconnaissance Wing, Alabama Air National Guard.

Captain Thomas R. Caldwell and Captain Fredrick A. Reid of the 48th Tactical Fighter Wing.

Staff Sergeant Thomas J. Moran of VMAQ-2, MAG-11, 3rd Marine Aircraft Wing.

Captain William D. Cronin, Captain Gary S. Dillon, Captain Kevin R. Dolvin, Captain William J. Hurley, Sergeant Kenneth T. Keller, Sergeant John R. Kilkus, Corporal Timothy W. Romei and Lance Corporal Thomas R. Adams of HMLA-267, USS *Okinawa* (LPH-3).

First Lieutenant Tommie W. Bates of the H&Hq B, 1/14 Field Artillery, 8th Infantry, 24th Infantry Division (Mechanized).

Specialist Robert A. Noonan of D Company, 1/505 Infantry (Airborne), 82nd Airborne Division.

MMFA Dale Jock of USS *La Salle* (AGF-3).

EM3 Daniel M. Jones of USS *Antietam* (CG-54).

God, send me to see such a company together again when need is.

Lord Howard of Effingham

Contents

Acknowledgments

This volume is dedicated to the brave Americans who lost their lives during Operation Desert Shield.

The text complies with voluntary constraints on the press requested by the Department of Defense. It contains thousands of facts, and errors are the sole responsibility of the author. The effort would have been impossible, however, without the generous help of many, including numerous American military units.

Among the many who helped, I would like to make special mention of Sergeant Dave Johnson of the 436th Military Airlift Wing. It is a privilege to know an outstanding American with the initiative and courage we want in our service members. Dave stands as a symbol for all the best.

I also thank the following:

In the world of public affairs: Don Black, Bob Bockman, Ken Carter, Richard M. Cole, Mike Cox, Scott Defries, Russell Egnor, Baxter "Ned" Ennis, A. C. Ewers, Bobbie Fiebel, Marvin Kusumoto, Edward "Ned" Lundquist, Thomas A. Sack, Carl Sahre, Susan Strednansky and Walter Thorp.

Among those on the ground: David Armijo, Michelle Curphey, Chris Fadness, Charles Kish, Kurt Koehler, William Morgan, Gilberto Ruiz, Rory M. Russell, Llewellyn Simms and Lanny Weldon.

Among those who fly and fight: William J. Begert, L. W. Crane, Matthew C. Davis, George Findlay, Dave Fundarek, Richard R. "Rick" Geffken, David A. Hinojoso, Thomas P. Loftus, Steve MacIsaac, Christopher Mardis, Lonny McClung, Michael G. Moffitt, Edward Renth, Marshall Siler, Joe A. Waltz and Stephanie A. Wells.

Among the fraternity: Michael M. Anselmo, Craig L. Baldwin, Mark Berent, Larry Bond, David F. Brown, Rick Burgess, Robert L. Burns, Lou Drendel, Richard A. Foster, Robert B. Greby, Michael Green, John Gresham, Joseph G. Handleman, Robert A. Pfannenschmidt, Rosario "Zip" Rausa, Eric Renth, Ricky Rizzo, the Gang at Roy's, Jim Sullivan and Wally Van Winkle.

The views expressed in this book are mine and do not necessarily reflect those of the US Air Force.

Robert F. Dorr

Chapter 1

Green Ramp

This is the story of the new breed of men and women in the US armed forces, thrust into crisis. Between August 1 and November 1, 1990, up to 240,000 of these new warriors were uprooted to a distant region of the globe and put to the test. It was the first time this new, different force was challenged with the prospect of an all-out, full-scale war against a formidable and determined adversary. The end of the story may not be known for a long time, but the start of it could always be pinpointed without doubt.

It begins where it always begins, at Green Ramp. Green Ramp is a tiny corner of Pope Air Force Base (AFB), North Carolina, itself an afterthought wedged into the Fort Bragg reservation near Fayetteville. Here, for generations, American paratroopers have practiced their trade and gone to war.

Wearing parachutes and surrounded by battle gear that seems to be strewn haphazardly but isn't, troopers of the 82nd Airborne Division stand, sit and lie in untidy rows on a shallow dirt slope running down from a tin barn to flat concrete where aircraft await. A few troopers are milling about. One has turned his heavy rucksack into a pillow and is snoring. Most are inspecting each other's gear, then inspecting it again, checking the straps under the groin and over the shoulder, which secure the T-10 main parachute and the chest-mounted reserve, checking the bright yellow static line with its silver metal hook. This is the final trust you can bestow upon another human being—to have your buddy scrutinize the straps, buckles and parachute you'll use to throw yourself out of a fast-moving airplane at low altitude, at night, in bad weather. These troopers have trust, they have a bond: the checking, the constant rechecking, goes on while the soldiers do what soldiers always do in the army, what they've done as long as we've had war. They hurry up and wait.

Dusk is gathering. A belch and a truncated whine erupt from a C-130E Hercules abortively running one engine on the flat concrete a hundred feet away. A slight breeze and a bit of a chill have come along to exacerbate the sweat these troopers have built up as they prepare and wait, prepare and wait. Murky, scudding clouds make this a lousy night—meaning the perfect night to rehearse a combat airdrop. It is 8:45 p.m. on the east coast of the United States, Wednesday, August 1, 1990. In an hour or two, a helicopter-supported, armored thrust by Iraqi forces will drive, blitzkrieg style, into the emirate of Kuwait, but the paratroopers of the 82nd Airborne Division do not yet know this.

I am at Green Ramp as part of an ongoing attempt to witness American armed forces where they live and work. These are not the armed forces many Americans think they recognize. They are new, and different, in ways few Americans appreciate.

New breed

From 1940 to 1975, we relied on a "citizen army," drawing its people from universal conscription, which served us well and made us all part of the same community—so that later in life, most of us remembered what it was like to wear a uniform, had some grasp of military terms and even had been shot at a couple times. War novels were peopled with unforgettable faces of yesteryear's people's militia—the boisterous Texan, the buttoned-down Ivy Leaguer, the drawling southern boy, the tormented Jew. When we needed them to, they charged machine gun nests. They also came home, continued on their lives, and—some of them, at least—rose up to run our corporations and our country.

Today's paratroopers at Green Ramp, who within hours will begin squinting at Kuwait on the map, have almost nothing in common with the very real soldiers, sailors and airmen who became the stuff of fiction in Irwin Shaw and Leon Uris. In 1975, the American people decided to purchase a professional, volunteer force. We

At 8:00 p.m., August 1, 1990, 82nd Airborne Division paratroopers at Green Ramp "hurry up and wait" to board a C–130 Hercules for an airdrop that will come after darkness falls. Each soldier wears a T-10C main back parachute, a yellow static line that will open the chute, a reserve chest chute, a rectangular M1950 weapons case for a Colt M16A2 rifle and an Alice pack, or rucksack, below the waist. These sol-diers are probably leaning against their Kevlar ballistic helmets (not seen). The 82nd is the first to go in a crisis, and Green Ramp is where it goes from. It is about 3 hours before Iraq's invasion of Kuwait, but a few more days will pass before Desert Shield sends paratroopers from Green Ramp to the Saudi desert.
Robert F. Dorr

got what we paid for, and again we were served well. We had it both ways. Our sons were no longer drafted. Our armed forces were no longer typical of the rest of us. We created a separate society, and during the free-spending Reagan years we financed it well—almost entirely on debt. Now, in mid 1990, the bills are coming in and we are telling the men and women in this separate society that their numbers, their opportunities, their careers will have to be sharply slashed to fix the budget mess.

On this August evening as Saddam Hussein is about to make himself a household word, the armed forces of the United States consist of 2,048,620 people, a decrease of 68,535 from a year earlier. This includes 734,641 in the Army, 578,907 in the Navy, 538,746 in the Air Force and 196,326 in the Marine Corps. Not included in the Pentagon's total are 38,005 in the Coast Guard, the fifth armed service. All told, this is the smallest force the United States has maintained in living memory.

In stark contrast to the troubled society they come from, the members of today's lean force are better educated, harder working, less well paid, almost entirely free of drugs and

Army paratroopers of the 82nd Airborne Division prepare to go. In the background is the Lockheed C-141B Starlifter, which is the Military Airlift Command's crucial workhorse in the rapid movement of people and equipment to the Middle East.

Though yellow ribbons will soon be flying from some American mailboxes and car antennas, the yellow in view here comes from the static lines that pull parachutes open following a jump. Robert F. Dorr

9

crime, and more likely to be steeped in the old-fashioned traits of sacrifice, commitment, patriotism. Almost all service members have a high school diploma and most, even in the lowest ranks, have some college. More belong to minorities. The Army is thirty-two percent black, nearly double the percentage in the population at large. Over ten percent of the force are women.

But the most important fact about this new force, a reality that must be confronted by the Pentagon brass, is the number who are married. In a lean, declining armed force where every measure of combat readiness must be eked out of too few people and too few resources, the

Commander of the C–5 and C–141 airlift wing at Travis AFB Colonel William J. Begert stands in front of a giant Lockheed C–5B Galaxy transport several weeks before Desert Shield. Begert wears the leather flight jacket that came into widespread use only in 1990 and that aroused controversy when the Air Force purchased large numbers to boost esprit de corps. A Vietnam veteran from Lewiston, Maine, Begert will soon begin employing his people and planes to build an air bridge between the United States and the steamy deserts of the Persian Gulf. Robert F. Dorr

number of married people has gone from about thirty percent to about sixty-five percent in fifteen years. The number of single parents has risen sharply. The number of service members married to each other has risen sharply. No other change has so profoundly affected our ability to remain ready for conflict and to have the wherewithal to fight and win.

Combat rehearsal

"We go," says Sergeant Bobbie Fiebel.

"Flying at low level is no picnic," warns Corporal Scott Defries. "You'd better grab a barf bag. You're going to get sick up there."

The crew of Lockheed C–130E Hercules 63-7882, call sign CHALK 1, is from the 50th Tactical Airlift Squadron, 314th Military Airlift Wing, temporarily here from Little Rock, Arkansas. C–130E 63-7882 is just one of the lizard-green transport planes pointed rear end toward these paratroopers—ramp down, propellers beginning to purr. The paratroopers file in twin rows up the lowered ramp, passing the two Air Force loadmasters who'll be working in the cargo bay. "Good to see you," one of the paratroopers says to a loadmaster. This is unusual. Though they train together, they have little real contact. Few of the paratroopers have ever had a long conversation with an airman. Few of the paratroopers have ever been up front to look at the flight deck of a C–130.

The four-engine, turboprop-powered Hercules is a success story. It has been in production since 1954, and 2,000 C–130s are hauling people and things around the world. Though not usually employed for long, over-the-ocean flights, Hercules is the best ship to transport people, equipment and weaponry within a combat zone. And Hercules is often the ship paratroopers throw themselves out of.

Tonight, with the paratroopers settled into rows of fold-down seats, the C–130 hurls aloft from Pope and climbs into the night. Some of the forty-odd troopers continue to check each other's gear. The two jump masters will guide, maybe even push, the troopers, who will go out of the aircraft at 130 knots (204 kilometers per hour), and then jump behind them. Two "safeties" will watch over the airdrop and do the housecleaning afterward, including reeling in and recovering static lines. In combat, the safeties would jump, too. Jump masters and safeties are among the Army's most experienced paratroopers, graduates of advanced jump school at Fort Bragg. Tonight's head jump master, a major, stands in the narrow row of the aircraft, helping another trooper to check her gear, again. The checking, the rechecking, is inbred.

Battle gear

These paratroopers wear a T-10C main parachute in a pack tray strapped to the back and secured by straps over shoulder and groin; its suspension lines and the chute canopy are olive-drab (OD) green in color—gone forever is the white parachute to attract enemy snipers. For jumps from higher altitude, the troopers might wear instead the MC1-1B main steerable parachute, which has a cutout section of canopy making it possible to steer by yanking on the risers.

As they did while waiting to board the aircraft, the paratroopers pay considerable attention to the long yellow static cord they carry, which will be hasped to a wire inside the aircraft and will pull their parachute open as they exit.

Positioned on each trooper's chest is a reserve parachute, which can be opened by hand in an emergency by yanking a silver metal D-ring. Like much of this jumping equipment, the reserve is bulky and awkward and the troopers have different opinions as to how much "insurance" this offers when jumping from 500 feet (155 meters).

A paratrooper's weapon is enclosed in a flat, burlaplike rectangular container called an M1950 weapons case. The soldier may have a Colt M16A2 5.56 millimeter air-cooled semiautomatic rifle weighing 8 pounds 12 ounces (2.75 kilograms); an M203, which is the same rifle with a grenade launcher; or an M60 machine gun. The soldier's head is encased in the lightweight "Fritz" Kevlar ballistic helmet. Other personal items and equipment hang in a heavy bag extending down from the waist and known as an Alice pack, rucksack or just plain ruck. Fatigue

uniform, jump boots or jungle boots, and even shoulder patches are all the battle dress utility (BDU) color of green-brown mottled camouflage, although the world will soon learn of lighter-colored BDUs intended for desert warfare.

CHALK 1 bores in over the North Carolina woods. C-130s at Pope, usually those stationed here with the 317th Wing but look-alikes for the visiting CHALK 1, drop Fort Bragg's paratroopers on training exercises day after day, year-around. Pope's 317th has a strong chance of being deployed on short notice if any rough stuff arises, because it's one of two wings in the Air Force equipped with the Adverse Weather Aerial Delivery System (AWADS) and Station Keeping Equipment (SKE). The AWADS ties an aircraft's radar into the navigation system, enabling the aircraft to fly for hours in poor weather, weave its way toward the drop zone at treetop level in defiance of an enemy's defenses

Richard R. Geffken, boom operator on a KC-135 R Stratotanker, learned of Iraq's invasion of Kuwait on August 2, 1990. At the time, he was on alert duty at Griffiss, keeping up round-the-clock readiness for nuclear war with the Soviet Union. By August 19, Geffken was arriving in a tanker in the sand-swept deserts of the Persian Gulf. Robert F. Dorr

and drop paratroopers with fine precision on the target. The other outfit with AWADS, also certain to be thrown into the breech if trouble starts, is the 435th Tactical Airlift Wing at Rhein-Main, Germany. Though supposedly *not* so equipped, our C–130E from Little Rock has this system, too; up on the front deck of CHALK 1

Shortly before Desert Shield began, airline captain Tom Loftus took a pay cut to leave one airline and begin flying for another. In his reserve role as a lieutenant colonel and the C–141B Starlifter instructor pilot with the 756th Military Airlift Squadron at Andrews AFB, Loftus volunteered to fly Desert Shield missions before his outfit was called to active duty on August 29, 1990. Taking a second pay cut to wear the Air Force uniform, Loftus felt pride at being a part of the largest airlift in history. Robert F. Dorr

where pilot, copilot, navigator and flight engineer sit in shadows over their instrument lights, the SKE console protrudes above the instrument panel looking like a bell-shaped Victorian clock or one of those old-fashioned home radio sets from the forties.

Countdown

As CHALK 1 rushes toward the drop zone, the mission becomes bumpy, gut wrenching. Inside the packed Hercules it is hot. Because a modern enemy may have shoulder-mounted missiles or radar-directed guns, the C–130E crew wracks the airplane into high-speed, "nap of the earth" flying at 300 feet (93 meters).

The usual way to avoid being sick in an aircraft is to look out, as far as you can, rather than focusing your eyes on the interior. But only one small window permits this, and through the window darkness has fallen over trees that seem to be passing by *above* the C–130.

Sergeant Matt Davis spent a year in the merchant marine before enlisting in the Air Force in January 1986. A "flying junkie" and loadmaster on a C–5B Galaxy with the 436th Military Airlift Wing, Davis was with his wife, Kelly, watching TV in his townhouse across the street from Dover AFB when he learned of the Iraqi invasion of Kuwait. Robert F. Dorr

The major holds up five fingers to tell everyone in the plane that we are 5 minutes from the drop.

"Five!" he bellows, though the sound of engines and rushing air is louder. The bright light bulb next to each door is still red. The drop is coming. A sharp, uplifting sensation is felt as the C-130 pops up to an altitude of 500 feet (155 meters), just long enough for the drop. The paratroopers stand in two rows now, their static lines hooked to the cable passing over their heads.

"Two minutes!" the major booms, holding up two fingers.

These are the critical seconds when CHALK 1 may be high enough for an enemy with radar and missiles to detect its approach, but by now it is probably too late. The loadmasters yank open the two side rear doors. Like an explosion, air rushes into the aircraft, sending particles of dust flying everywhere inside the ship. Many troopers who have no vision impairment wear securely fastened glasses because of this flying storm of tiny particles. A creek bed is visible in the darkness not far below, a visual checkpoint.

Airdrop

In combat, an enemy below may be ready to engage these troopers while they still fall from the sky, or the moment they hit hard ground. The troopers must think not only about how they will plummet into the sky, but what they will do the moment they're down. At the 1 minute mark, the major signals again and the light next to each door turns green.

"Go!" the major bellows.

One by one, the paratroopers leap into the door jambs and hurl themselves out. A trooper's own strength is enough to get about 6 inches up and 36 inches out of the narrow door, where the airstream and the 70 pound (32 kilogram) weight of the equipment will combine with gravity to do the rest.

Watching all this happen, watching one trooper leave the aircraft on each side every 1.5 seconds, is a kind of anticlimax. A split second of worry occurs when one man hesitates, but he is gone in a glimpse. Except for safeties and loadmasters, CHALK 1 is abruptly empty. Lines are reeled in, doors are closed, the aircraft descends again and within minutes the C-130 Hercules will be settling down at Pope.

The night landing is impressive after I move up front in CHALK 1 and look over the AWADS console at approaching runway lights. Corporal Defries had exaggerated. Although the flying was rough, no one, not even I, needed a barf bag.

Back at the drop zone, the troopers will go through a brief night combat exercise, then board waiting trucks to return home. They're out in the North Carolina woods now, out of sight, but they linger in my mind. Most are young. Most are bright. Students of history, they are not. Few have known of paratroopers before who jumped into Sicily, Normandy, Korea and Vietnam. Few have a sense for history or the curiosity that will bring them, in the difficult days to follow, to remember that this is what they happened to be doing at the moment Saddam Hussein was invading Iraq.

Dramatis personae

Where were you?

If you're old enough, you may remember with painstaking exactness what was happening in your life the day Pearl Harbor was attacked or President John F. Kennedy was shot. Most people do not remember what they were doing in the late hours of August 1, 1990, East Coast time, when Iraq overran Kuwait.

Afterward, when there was no going back to change any part of those difficult days of August, September and October 1990, when we had sent 240,000 American men and women to sand-swept deserts and troubled waters in the Persian Gulf to determine the shape of our world for the remainder of the century, only a few who participated remembered where they were when it started.

Chris Fadness, age nineteen, raised in Hood River, Oregon, is in a 7-Eleven store along the cluttered boulevard in Fayetteville, North Carolina, not far from the low-flying CHALK 1, picking up chips and soft drinks and thinking about a coming barracks inspection and a promotion due to him in another month. He has a car payment coming up. Slim, tussle-haired, a little shy,

Private First Class Chris Fadness, his head just visible protruding from the first of four M551 Sheridan tanks belonging to the 82nd Airborne Division, prepares to drive his tank aboard a C–5B Galaxy during an airlift movement. At age nineteen, Fadness was already a veteran of Operation Just Cause in Panama when he found himself uprooted to Saudi Arabia in August 1990. Robert F. Dorr

Whether for Panama or Saudi Arabia, arrivals and departures of American service members are touching moments for families, spouses and especially children. Major Matt Davis of the 82nd Airborne Division would like to spend more time with his son but will do so when duty permits. Department of Defense

cheerful, Fadness is a private first class and driver of an M551 Sheridan light tank in the 82nd Airborne Division. Eight months ago, during fighting at Tocumen airfield in Panama, rifle bullets punched two circular dents into the front of his tank a few inches from his head.

John M. Gordon, age forty-four, a native of Wilmington, Delaware, is lounging around in his modest Houston, Texas, home chatting with his wife, Judy, about their three children, resisting the urge to reach for one of the cigarettes he still smokes and reflecting upon a recent layoff from his full-time job in computer sales. With thinning hair, the start of a paunch and a strictly amateur swing on his neighborhood tennis team, Gordon, is a major in the reserves and aircraft commander of a C-5A Galaxy with the 68th Military Airlift Squadron at Kelly Field in San Antonio, Texas, 100 miles (160 kilometers) from his home. Gordon is one of the few reservists who is a pilot in the reserves but not in civilian life. Previously, he flew the C-130 Hercules.

Michelle Curphey, age nineteen, from Manchester, New Hampshire, is driving her trouble-prone, seven-year-old Honda Civic along Interstate 95 from Savannah, Georgia, after an early evening computer class, thinking about an upcoming barracks inspection and an impending visit by her widowed father. A trim woman with finely chiseled features, Curphey is a private first class and a wheeled vehicle maintenance assistant on a High Mobility Multipurpose Wheeled Vehicle (HMMWV), or Humm-Vee, tactical vehicle with the 24th Infantry Division (Mechanized) at Fort Stewart, Georgia.

Richard R. "Rick" Geffken, age twenty-two, is spending a quiet evening in his split-level, two-bedroom, New England style house at the foot of a sloping meadow in Bridgewater, New York, with his wife, Stephanie. Geffken, who studied premed for a year at a small private college before joining the Air Force to become a refueling boom operator on a KC-135R Stratotanker, is an airman first class. Stephanie Geffken, age twenty-four, also an airman first class, is an environmental support specialist in an Air Force civil engineering unit and would normally be among the first to go overseas in any deployment, but the couple's first child is expected within six weeks. Also on Geffken's mind is the small auto body business he runs on the side. Rick and Stephanie Geffken are both leaving the service soon: "Our pay status is my major gripe," says Geffken. Meanwhile, Geffken is scheduled to go on alert with the 41st Air Refueling Squadron of the 416th Bomb Wing at Griffiss AFB, New York, beginning tomorrow, August 2, 1990. This means being part of a tanker crew remaining at the ready, on base, to be launched within minutes together with the base's B-52G Stratofortress bombers in the event of a sudden, transpolar war with the Soviet Union. Geffken will learn of Iraq's overrunning Kuwait only after reporting to the alert facility.

Airlift fliers

Thomas P. Loftus, age forty-three, a Chicago, Illinois, native, is far from the white-trimmed, cedar, riverfront house in Annapolis, Maryland, where he lives with wife, Susan, and four daughters, though he is thinking of Susan's plan to resume her interrupted career as a supervisory registered nurse. After Loftus rose through the ranks to become a Boeing 727 captain with Eastern Air Lines, labor problems led him to start again for less pay as second officer with another airline that he likes very much, United. Loftus is on an airline layover—later, he will not remember where—viewing cable TV in his hotel when he learns of the Iraqi invasion. Silver-haired, a sports addict with a love for handball and skiing, Loftus is a lieutenant colonel in the reserves doing part-time duty as an aircraft commander and instructor pilot of a C-141B Starlifter with the 756th Military Airlift Squadron at Andrews AFB, Maryland.

William J. Begert, age forty-four, is going about the business of running the 60th Military Airlift Wing at Travis AFB, California, while finding a little time to spend with his wife, Joanne, son, William, and daughter, Katherine. Relaxed and youngish looking, Begert is a colonel who graduated from the Air Force Academy and flew tiny O-2 forward air control planes in Vietnam. He now commands the only wing equipped with both the giant C-5 Galaxy and the C-141B

Starlifter—the two aircraft that will be needed most if a major air bridge has to be built to a distant land.

Mike Nevatt is a "grape," or fuel chief, of the 140 man Division V-4 aboard the carrier USS *Dwight D. Eisenhower* (CVN-69). Nevatt's job: leading others struggling with fuel hoses 2½ inches in diameter, which, even without JP-5 jet fuel coursing through them, are heavy and cumbersome. A senior chief petty officer, Nevatt works part of the time far below the seventh deck in Pump Room No. 2, a maze of pumps, valves and ducting supported on steel grates. *Ike*

American forces in Saudi Arabia and elsewhere in the Middle East fell under General H. Norman Schwarzkopf, Commander in Chief of US Central Command. Normally headquartered in Florida, Schwarzkopf's command was moved to Saudi Arabia during Operation Desert Shield. US Army/R. F. Roederer

and its carrier battle group are in the western Mediterranean, nearing the end of the long Med cruise, and Nevatt and his buddies are glad to be on the verge of going home.

Matthew C. "Matt" Davis, age twenty-four, is at home in his townhouse across from Dover AFB, Delaware, helping his wife, Kelly, to make the chocolate chip cookies he takes on long trips. A phone call tells Davis that his C-5B Galaxy outfit, the 436th Military Airlift Wing at Dover, will be on increased alert status. Davis is concerned that Kelly's car has broken down and he may not have time to repair it. He is a loadmaster on a C-5B and joined the Air Force more than four years ago. "Up until Desert Shield, I saw this as a job," admits Davis. "When I joined the Air Force I never dreamed that I might get caught up in a war. Never until the beginning of this thing."

The real thing

It is not always easy to remember when a thing begins. As midnight brings the start of August 2, weary from the CHALK 1 flight, I drop into an air-conditioned room at the Howard Johnson, switch on cable news TV and hear something about trouble in Kuwait City. A half-hour later, newscasters are speaking by phone to somebody in Kuwait City who talks of intense fighting raging around the emir's palace.

Air conditioning and television. In the difficult days ahead, they will assume a strange and new importance while many of us learn for the first time about paratroopers, C-130s, Humm-Vees, desert BDUs and even chemical warfare gear. It is not easy to know when a thing begins, but if it means rapid deployment of American forces overseas in time of crisis, it is always easy to know where. It begins at Green Ramp.

At 2:00 a.m. on August 2, instead of getting some sleep, because of that sharp jolt inside that warns maybe it's happening *right now*, I take a long drive through Fayetteville, back through Bragg, up to the Pope gate to look through the fence. But it is the wrong time. Though just about all of Kuwait has fallen, Green Ramp is empty. Empty but for a pair of Air Force maintenance personnel, sitting on the slope in the darkness, talking idly. Nothing is happening. Not yet.

It will. On another night just eight months ago, the tin barn, gnarled trees and gentle dirt slope facing the Pope flight line were crusted with ice, the temperature was below freezing, the runways were coated with a perilous slick and a frigid wind was blowing as the paratroopers kitted up and climbed aboard aircraft for a 5 hour flight that would end with a combat drop in the tropics. "That time," says Bobbie Fiebel, ". . . I remember the ammunition." It was the sight of vast amounts of ammunition being loaded that told them this was the real thing. Two thousand men dropped into Panama on December 20, 1989, in Operation Just Cause, among them tonight's major aboard CHALK 1, Bobbie Fiebel and Chris Fadness.

Now, another few days will pass before the start of Desert Shield, but when it begins, some participants will be veterans of that brief tropical brush fire in Panama. It always begins at Green Ramp because the 82nd Airborne Division always goes first.

Chapter 2

Air

On July 25, 1990, after meeting with Iraq's Saddam Hussein, American ambassador April C. Glaspie wrote in an "immediate" cable to the State Department that Iraq's military build-up along the Kuwaiti border was cosmetic, posturing, a show of force—that Hussein would not actually *invade* the sovereign and independent emirate of Kuwait.

Glaspie said little during her face-to-face meeting with Hussein that day. Summoned on short notice, she'd had no time to seek instructions. The Iraqi leader did most of the talking, fomenting about his dispute over oil prices and other issues with his next-door neighbor. Glaspie did, however, assure Hussein that the United States did not want to become involved in an Iraqi-Kuwaiti dispute.

In Washington's Foggy Bottom, during a summer of torturous humidity, many who normally would read Glaspie's cable were away at the beach. A few, however, scrutinized the text, and wondered why Glaspie had left out the customary final paragraph offering a personal assessment. A few reached for alarm bells. An analyst in a Washington intelligence agency keyboarded a memo warning that Iraq was unpredictable and Kuwait indefensible. "Kuwait would not be able to hold out against a determined attack," she wrote. At another agency, a Navy lieutenant cautioned others that Iraq would not be constrained by rules of behavior that bind other nations.

At the end of July, Iraq moved at least 200,000 troops up to the Kuwaiti frontier. Several hundred Iraqi tanks shimmered on the parched, gritty sands, their cannons pointed at Kuwaiti refineries and rigs.

Glaspie, a Mideast diplomatic veteran, had a vacation coming. She departed Baghdad in late July—a catastrophic choice of timing.

Iraqi onslaught

At 2:00 a.m., Thursday, August 2, 1990, tanks, troops and helicopters belonging to the armed forces of Iraq burst across the border into the thinly defended Persian Gulf emirate of Kuwait, the start of a full-scale invasion. It was the worst time of year for fighting on the desert, the air torrid and miserable at 105 degrees Fahrenheit (41 degrees Celsius) in the crisp, clear darkness. In isolated locations, Kuwaiti defenders *did* fight. Battles sputtered and flared. Here and there, an antitank rocket or a burst of tracer fire sparked and flashed in the night. But the main force of Iraqi tanks was soon roaring down a six-lane highway toward Kuwait City.

Iraq's Soviet-built MiG fighters rattled windows in the capital, and the vanguard of the 140,000 man invasion force began taking Kuwait City street by street, overrunning the Interior Ministry and the Foreign Ministry. Snatches on the phone from tourists in Kuwait City, played "live" on cable TV, told the outside world of gunfire and fighting at scattered points in the capi-

If the United States was going to build an air bridge to the Saudi desert, the bulk of the work had to fall to the Lockheed C-141B Starlifter. Lizard-green C-141B 65-0275 from the 437th Military Airlift Wing at Charleston, South Carolina, was showing its stuff a few weeks before the Kuwait invasion. The C-141B was an unsung hero of the skies, but it was growing old. A lifetime of 45,000 flying hours had been foreseen, and some C-141Bs had already passed the 38,000 figure when Desert Shield began. Joseph G. Handelman, DDS

tal. When daylight arrived, a European businessman in a Kuwait hotel took a few seconds of videotape that was later shown, repeatedly, on every major television network—an Iraqi T-72 tank, firing a round from its heavy gun in the city center, a squadron of Iraqi helicopters alighting in the capital like an Orwellian swarm of bugs.

The Mil Mi-8 helicopters may have carried elite Iraqi special operations troopers who attacked vulnerable Kuwaiti nodes, such as broadcast centers and microwave facilities.

The other heavyweight of the American airlift effort was the Lockheed C-5 Galaxy, the largest aircraft in US service. A Galaxy could carry four M551 Sheridan tanks, a Humm-Vee battlefield vehicle and seventy-two soldiers. This lizard-green C-5B belongs to the 436th Military Airlift Wing at Dover AFB, *commanded by Colonel Michael G. "Mike" Moffitt. When a Galaxy crashed at Ramstein on August 29, 1990, other Galaxy pilots continued taking off and landing over the wreckage, keeping up the flow of people and equipment to Desert Shield.* Robert F. Dorr

Some may have descended on the royal family's Dasman Palace where fighting was fierce and the Kuwaiti emir's brother was among those who died resisting the onslaught. The emir was evacuated by land—not by helicopter, as widely reported—and whisked to refuge in Saudi Arabia. In 12 hours, by early afternoon, August 2, 1990, Iraqi forces were mopping up scattered pockets of resistance, having pulled off a power grab so wickedly brilliant that almost no one had realized how obvious it was, all along. Like a forbidden fruit beckoning to be plucked, Kuwait—ripe, tender, a little flabby—had been taken. Saddam Hussein commanded a fifth of the world's known oil reserves.

President George Bush immediately ordered an embargo of all trade with Iraq and began asking other nations to join the United States in slapping down economic sanctions on Iraq and its assets.

For Americans, who were not good at geography anyway, it was time to reach for the books. Our enemy was Russia. Our friend was Israel. Our rapid deployment forces trained in desert warfare to thwart a Soviet thrust into the Persian Gulf. Right? In the bloody eight-year war between Iraq and Iran, we had spoken of being on no one's side, but—quietly, at least—we had hoped Iraq would stick the screws to those ayatollahs over in Iran. Right?

Everything was turned upside down. In the Soviet Union and Eastern Europe, communism had collapsed and the threat had shriveled. Israel might seem an ally to some Americans, although no defense treaty had even been inked, but it was merely a spectator to the blitzkrieg that had come down over Kuwait like a tidal wave. Very suddenly, Iraq had gobbled up one neighbor and now appeared capable of devouring another—Saudi Arabia.

Americans had to do plenty of rethinking, plenty fast. For years, apologists for Israel had complained about Saudi Arabia using petrodollars to arm itself to the teeth with F-15 and Tornado jets, E-3 airborne warning and control system (AWACS) planes, and M1 Abrams tanks. Thanks to Israeli lobbying, an impression had lodged in American minds that the Saudis had plenty of military might, more than they needed.

The complaint, and the impression, were wrong. Saudi Arabia had 68,000 people under arms, Iraq a million. The Saudis had a few hundred main battle tanks, the Iraqis 5,500—more tanks than Hitler used to overrun the continent of Europe in an armored lightning war. If Saudi Arabia was far less well defended than Americans had been told, how could the Saudis protect themselves any better than the Kuwaitis had done?

Were Americans going to be needed in the Middle East, in a role they had never envisioned? Not to fight the Russians, not to defend Israel, not even to stand up to the ayatollahs in nearby Iran; Americans might instead have to embark, now, to defend one Arab state from another—Saudi Arabia from Iraq. It was crazy. It was happening.

But before it could happen, the Saudis had to be persuaded that they needed defending. In the first of many moves revealing that Defense Secretary Dick Cheney had more influence than Secretary of State Jim Baker, President George Bush instructed Cheney to fly to Jedda to talk with King Fahd.

Going into the weekend of August 4 and 5, 1990, Bush orchestrated diplomatic and military moves. The president was furious over the Iraqi takeover of Kuwait. With Cheney and Chairman of the Joint Chiefs General Colin Powell, Bush agonized over courses of action. Probably as early as Saturday, August 4, the chief executive made up his mind that a deployment of American forces would take place, not on a modest scale as it might first appear, but on a magnitude never before attempted.

Baker drew the important but second-level job of flying to Turkey to seek support. Turkey, too, bordered on Iraq, and at the time of the invasion, American F-111E Aardvark fighter-bombers normally stationed in England had been working out at Turkey's Incirlik airfield. In fact, ten days before the invasion, the 20th Tactical Fighter Wing had lost F-111E 68-0066 when the two-man crew ran into trouble 62

miles (100 kilometer) from Incirlik and ejected safely.

Baker went to Moscow to solicit Soviet support. Between August 2 and August 6, a hectic American quest for backing in other capitals led to a diplomatic triumph. The United States, which usually stood alone, drummed up a unanimous endorsement from the United Nations (UN) Security Council, token support from many countries and significant help from a few countries—Egypt was one—with the courage to put aside past grudges and confront Iraq.

Saudi request

Dick Cheney's mission to Saudi Arabia could be looked at in different ways. American soldiers, sailors, airmen, and marines in that part of the world came under US Central Command (Centcom), headquartered in Florida but responsible for the Middle East, commanded by Army general H. Norman Schwarzkopf. But blunt, crusty Stormin' Norman couldn't command so much as a buck private in somebody else's country unless he was "invited" to. "We had damned well made up our mind," says a staffer who accompanied Cheney. "We were going to put our troops in there. If the Saudis felt threatened and wanted our help, which was the way it turned out, that was fine. If they didn't, we were going to remind them that we had been helping *them* for years and it was payback time."

As Cheney himself described the mission:

"On August 6, four days after the invasion of Kuwait, I briefed King Fahd about the threat from Iraq and the military capabilities we could provide to help deter further Iraqi aggression and to help defend Saudi Arabia. King Fahd's courageous decision to request foreign assistance speaks to the seriousness of the situation.

Commanded by Colonel John McBroom, the 1st Tactical Fighter Wing at Langley AFB has long had a commitment to be available to the Middle East region handled by US Central Command. F–15C Eagles like aircraft 83–035, were the first to deploy to the Persian Gulf region, departing Langley on August 7, 1990. Craig L. Baldwin

King Fahd . . . spoke of his faith in our commitment to help defend his country, to stay until the job was done, and when the job was done and we were asked to leave, in fact, to leave."

When he made the decision to send American men and women to the Persian Gulf, George Bush did so in a conference room at Camp David, his hideaway in Maryland's Catoctin Mountain, though he was to spend much of August at his vacation home in Maine. Bush ordered the deployment of US forces on August 7, 1990. Operation Desert Shield was to have four goals:

1. Deter and, if necessary, repel further Iraqi aggression.

2. Effect the withdrawal of all Iraqi forces from Kuwait.

3. Restore the legitimate government of Kuwait.

4. Protect the lives of American citizens.

These were the Four Points to be dredged up again and again by Washington spokespeople in the weeks ahead, but some felt the real US purpose was to eradicate Saddam Hussein. Not everybody thought this was a bad idea.

The *H*-word

Almost immediately, it became known that fourteen American oil workers in Kuwait were unaccounted for. No one wanted to use the *H*-word, because memories of the Carter administration being paralyzed by a hostage issue were well implanted and vivid. It was becoming apparent that thousands of Americans in Iraq and Kuwait were in jeopardy. Among expatriates in occupied Kuwait alone were 3,000 Americans, 3,000 Britons and 4,000 Turks. It was worse for other nations. Some, like India,

These F-15C Eagles of the 1st Tactical Fighter Wing are in a revetment at the principal American air base in eastern Saudi Arabia. The aircraft in the foreground, number 82–0018, has air conditioning connected to cool its internal systems, and one result is a fogged-up canopy. The aircraft in the background, number 83–0026, has just raised its "barn door" speed brake and the pilot is now ready to taxi out. Robert F. Dorr

26

SSgt Eugene McCullough
SrA Tyrone Tillery

2018

SSgt Donald Bowman
Sgt Bradley Schellhaaf

3026

had tens of thousands of "guest workers" in Kuwait who were now, whether anybody wanted to use the word or not, hostages.

The saga of American and other foreign civilians detained and mistreated under Saddam Hussein's regime is worth a volume in itself, never far from our story of Americans in uniform. The problem was bigger and more serious than anyone had guessed. At first, we had a glimmer of hope that innocents might be allowed to depart unharmed, and toward this goal officials in Washington spoke of them gingerly—but after less than a week, George Bush authorized his administration to call them hostages and began using the word himself.

The first, tentative steps were taken to increase the US military presence in the Middle East. The carrier battle group headed up by USS *Independence* (CV-62) was at steam in the

While Americans fanned out across the desert, the airlift gained momentum. Civilian charters, like this Lockheed L–1011, flew alongside military C–5s and C–141Bs. Using the call sign AM TRAM 188 HEAVY, this L–1011 passes in front of a waiting KC–135R tanker at Griffiss AFB, arriving to pick up Persian Gulf bound Army troops from nearby Fort Drum. Robert F. Dorr

Indian Ocean and was ordered westward to the Persian Gulf region. Aboard *Independence*, Carrier Air Wing, Two, commanded by Captain Jay B. Yakeley III, was honed to a fighting edge, ready to lash out with Hornet and Intruder attack ships and cover them with F-14 Tomcats. A similar force was embarked aboard USS *Eisenhower* in the eastern Mediterranean—but although not distant in miles, *Ike* was in the wrong body of water to be immediately helpful.

In Operation Desert Shield, Bush and his advisors were planning a military response far larger than anyone imagined. Had the sands of the Persian Gulf region produced macadamia nuts rather than petroleum, things might have been different. But in 1989 alone, the United States consumed 17 billion barrels of oil per day, and only 8 billion were produced at home, the remaining 9 billion being imported. Almost 2½ million barrels of Organization of Petroleum Exporting Countries (OPEC) petroleum per day were flowing into America's cars. A sizable proportion of this imported oil is from Kuwait and, yes, Iraq.

Behind the scenes, while remaining on vacation rather than rushing to Washington, Bush planned the massive deployment of US forces largely in secret, its announced purpose being the Four Points.

First step in the deployment began on August 7, 1990, when the 2,300 man "ready brigade" of the 82nd Airborne Division was uprooted. Green Ramp at Pope finally became a beehive, as expected.

In Fayetteville, a few miles from Green Ramp, Private First Class Chris Fadness of the 82nd Airborne had just returned from the motor pool when his charge of quarters (CQ) told him that the paratroopers were going. "Sure enough," Fadness recalls, "it was all over the news that evening. My friends and I were debating whether or not we would be going and after almost an hour of debate, came to the conclusion we would. We believed we would be spearheading an invasion."

On the night the 82nd was activated, Fadness was picking up a pal. "A buddy of mine, Jason Kish, had called from the Fayetteville airport asking me for a ride, as he had just returned from leave. I guess it was about 12:30 a.m. or so. I went and picked him up, and as we returned to Fort Bragg we noticed every parking lot was full. We knew right then that the entire division had been alerted during our short absence. It was kind of scary, as it hit us that this was it. We felt so unprepared!"

This may be modesty speaking. In fact, the M551 Sheridan tanks of Fadness' outfit, and the people, were ready.

Paratroopers, clothed in desert garb, boarded C-141B Starlifters for the 15 hour journey to the Saudi deserts. The paratroopers' first job was to form defenses at the principal air base in Saudi Arabia—the airfield built by Americans in World War II, expanded since then to become the country's largest, and now the main US staging area.

On August 7, Operation Desert Shield was publicly announced. Rapid deployment forces would be the first to go. These were the troops and weapons that had been tagged to go first in any Mideast crisis. This meant 82nd Airborne paratroopers, the first of other army units and F-15C Eagles of the 1st Tactical Fighter Wing at Langley AFB, which—vastly outnumbered— would have to gain air superiority and hold it if fighting began at an early stage.

On August 7, emotions were high at Langley, near Hampton in the Virginia tidewater, when Colonel John M. "Boomer" McBroom's 1st Tactical Fighter Wing's 27th and 71st squadrons began leaving for Saudi Arabia on just hours' notice. The word had been out, in fact, since the previous day when post exchanges and local grocers suddenly found themselves selling out of such staples as toothpaste, lip balm and bath soap. Leaves were canceled. The crowds in restaurants, bars and shopping malls abruptly thinned out. It was a sudden and dramatic uprooting, though the story was to be repeated again and again at other bases. Airman Kimberly Newburg, the twenty-year-old crew chief of F-15C Eagle 82-0021, was glad her training was about to be put to use.

Few remembered it, but the idea of maintaining a permanent armed force was a recent

one in American history, dating only to 1940. Before that, only a skeleton crew had practiced the profession of arms in peacetime. Because memory is short, merchants had even forgot *why* we now maintained armed forces; a pesky minority complained that deploying troops overseas was bad for business. Most supported the men and women in uniform, however, including a laundromat owner who fashioned a crude sign that said God bless all of you. Sales of a bumper sticker with the American flag and the warning THESE COLORS DON'T RUN shot skyward.

Airmen (a term the Air Force uses for male *and* female personnel) in Langley's "mobility units," charged with rapid deployment to the gulf, began boarding cargo planes while Mc-Broom's F-15C Eagle fighters hurtled aloft. A contingent of Air Force Security Police went with them. These airmen were supposed to have gas mask, hood, rubber gloves and a charcoal-lined suit just in case Iraq got serious about chemical warfare, but none were yet available. The units were briefed to expect 120 degree Fahrenheit (49 degrees Celsius) heat and blowing sand by day, frigid temperatures at night. This was exactly two-thirds accurate and one-third dead wrong. It did *not* get cold at night in August in Saudi Arabia—in fact, the heat was debilitating—but there were plenty of other

The 336th Tactical Fighter Squadron, part of the 4th Tactical Fighter Wing at Seymour Johnson AFB, was the first unit with a Desert Shield commitment to operate the dual-role F–15E Strike Eagle, capable of both air-to-air and air-to-ground action. Strike Eagles such as 87–204 began deploying to the gulf region on August 9, 1990. Craig L. Baldwin

Next page

Slated for duties in US Central Command's area of responsibility in the Mideast, the 363rd Tactical Fighter Wing at Shaw AFB was equipped with F–16C/D Fighting Falcon jet fighters, one of which is seen here just before Desert Shield. The 363rd deployed to the Persian Gulf region beginning on August 8, 1990. Craig L. Baldwin

The Boeing E–3 Sentry AWACS, used to detect enemy activity and guide other American warplanes over the battlefield, was no stranger to Saudi Arabia. By the time this E–3 was dispatched in August 1990, others had been routinely operating from air bases in the Saudi deserts, in both American and Saudi colors, for several years. US Air Force

Past experience in the Saudi desert

In 1983, Edward Renth, a retired Air Force lieutenant colonel, used his civil engineer's credentials to do the survey for a security fence around the full 30 mile (48 kilometer) perimeter of Dhahran air base. It was the period when an embarrassment of too many petrodollars, too fast, propelled the Saudis to haste in their ambitious Infrastructure Program—building highways and hospitals, creating new cities out of desert and constructing two desalinization plants, one on each coast. A people new to modernization, the Saudis were enthralled with high-tech. At Dhahran, Renth was instructed to install motion detectors and noise recorders as part of the security setup around the fence. "It didn't work too well because of too many wild camels around there," he said.

Renth lived in the town of Al Khobar, 3 miles (4.82 kilometers) south of Dhahran. Al Khobar is on the gulf; it was once a fishing village but was now built up, with sea front hotels. "But there were few tourists," said Renth. "To be there, you had to have a work visa."

In a larger project, Renth worked with Saudi air force major Bandar Bin Sultan, project officer, on Peace Hawk V. The hard-working Saudi major, young but eager, was a pilot who had been trained at Randolph Field, Texas. He was also one of 3,000 to 5,000 princes in what must be the world's most populous royal family. Almost a decade later, when Desert Shield began, Prince Sultan Bandar was Saudi Arabia's ambassador to Washington.

Peace Hawk V was an enormous military aid project that gave Saudi Arabia 150 Northrop F–5E Tiger fighters and three new air bases, all provided "turnkey" with 506 quarters at each, commissary, library, movie theater—"just like an American air base," according to Renth. The Americans furnished everything down to knives, forks and spoons.

Renth: "I started out at Khamis Mushayt near the Yemen border in mountains at elevation 7,200 near Red Sea. We built almost an entire base over top of what the British had built originally. A squadron of Lightnings was there and we moved fifty F–5Es in. At Taif, 40 miles [64 kilometers] southeast of Mecca, we built another military base, another fifty fighters, 506 quarters and so on. We provided it all—hangars, ranks, wash racks, fuel facilities—to create a modern fighter wing base." The Peace Hawk V program cost no less than $5 billion.

Renth remembers the type of conditions that would greet the Americans of Desert Shield. "I motored across the desert with a convoy to Khamis. Our route was Dhahran-Riyadh-Taif-Khamis, following goat tracks and goat trails. A highway had just been constructed by the Germans.

"What's it like on the desert? The Riyadh-Taif leg of the trip was damned hot. There was no shade anyplace. The thermometer said 95 degrees Fahrenheit [35 degrees Celsius] inside the truck (*with* air conditioning) but it was 135 degrees [Fahrenheit; 57 degrees Celsius] outside.

"I'd just bought a brand new pair of foam rubber shoes. With my right foot on the truck's accelerator, the floorboards were so hot I thought something was wrong with my foot. It took me a while to realize that the sole had melted, leaving a big lump on the instep of my shoe and nothing on the outside of my foot.

"So much sand blew across the two-lane blacktop road, you couldn't tell where road was and where desert was. You'd see nothing but sand and a black spot ahead in the distance, and *that* was the rest of the road. It's different now—three lanes each side going both ways, a real superhighway. I was even told that the Saudis had imported flora and fauna from the American western desert and planted it on both sides of the road to keep sand from blowing on the highway."

Renth, interviewed in August 1990 as Desert Shield was in high gear, wondered how things would go for the Desert Shield's warriors if things continued into November. "The desert gets cold in winter, down below freezing sometimes. In November, it be hot in the daytime but down into the forties at night. Our kids out there on the desert will need some heavier clothing."

things Americans didn't know about Saudi Arabia.

What they did know was that Saudi was a land of contrast. It became more so: outside the main airfield, Saudi women shielded themselves beneath black head covers while American women armed and maintained jet fighters wearing T-shirts and no bras. Airmen such as Kimberly Newburg, however, could not leave their immediate work area without male escort, could not—at first—use an exercise gym available to men and were required to enter some buildings by the rear door. In imposing these rules on American women, American officers believed they were honoring Saudi sensibilities.

Desert conditions

A survey showed that young people in America ranked seventeenth behind those in other nations in their knowledge of geography. To a handful of Americans in an older generation, Saudi Arabia was neither strange nor unfamiliar. The new breed, however, had never been in such a place before and were unprepared for the climate or the conditions.

The Saudi desert. In early August 1990, volunteering to fly an airlift mission with his reserve squadron, Lieutenant Colonel Tom Loftus made two trips to Saudi airfields. Under the rules, he cannot name them. "The first time I landed my C–141, I stepped out of the aircraft and looked around. It was early evening. The temperature was 85 degrees Fahrenheit [29 degrees Celsius]. This was not too uncomfortable. If you were staying over, you could take care of your business and end up at a little place where you could sit outdoors and drink a martini."

In fact, as the airlift heightened, you no longer had any place to stay over or to get a martini. If you went *downrange*—the term that quickly came into use for proceeding into the

During an unusually quiet moment, fog takes shape over the principal US flight line in Saudi Arabia, obscuring the two principal airlifters, the C–141B Starlifter and C–5B Galaxy. Robert F. Dorr

39

Desert Shield area—you might not get any crew rest until you found your way back to Europe. And if you landed at midday, conditions were much less tolerable; the sun was hottest at 10:00 a.m.

Loftus: "The second time I landed my C-141 in Saudi Arabia, it was early afternoon. I stepped out and I thought the airplane in front of me had fired up his engines and had gotten too close and hit us with his exhaust. I looked at the airplane and realized that I couldn't hear his engines so he wasn't running them. I had been hit with this sudden blast of raw heat as if it came from a furnace. It hit you and it stayed there and you were stuck with it. It was overpowering. It was typical at that time of day for the temperature to reach 120 degrees Fahrenheit [49 degrees Celsius]."

As late as August 8, 1990, it remained unclear just how big Desert Shield really *was*,

The airlift of troops and equipment was staged through air bases in Europe, where a pool of aircrews waited to pick up cargo planes arriving from the United States and continue the journey to the Middle East. These C-5B Galaxy crew members, with Sergeant Matt Davis in the center, have just completed the 8 hour flight from Dover to Torrejon and are preparing to turn the Galaxy over to a new crew, which will continue downrange. Robert F. Dorr

though one clue was forthcoming when officers asked reporters to stop naming bases, altogether—even the main airfield. Early on, at least fifteen airfields had been chosen for use by American forces, and press rules now forbade naming them, even the obvious ones. In starting Desert Shield, President George Bush had adopted a principle fast becoming a part of US doctrine: If the United States was to commit forces overseas, the forces must be overwhelming.

Major airlift

To get Americans into place, the burden of responsibility fell, first, on the Air Force. That service's new chief of staff, General Michael J. Dugan, once flew prop-driven A-1 Skyraiders in Southeast Asia—in fact, he bailed out of one over Laos—but Dugan was also a negotiator, adept at getting support for the military's urgent business with Congress, the press and the public. Military Airlift Command (MAC) chief General Hansford T. "H. T." Johnson was another gentleman-warrior, as well as the first graduate of the US Air Force Academy at Colorado Springs, Colorado, to attain four-star rank. Strategic Air Command's (SAC's) General John T. "Jack" Chain was a hard-charging advocate of air power, including the controversial B-2 stealth bomber, and also knew of the importance of the little-recognized tankers used to refuel other warplanes in flight. Dugan, Johnson and Chain were, to use a Pentagon term, *key players.*

Desert Shield was to prove a personal tragedy for Dugan and a challenge for Johnson, who was also responsible for sealift as the boss of the recently created Transportation Command. As Americans began packing up and pulling out, Johnson told the press that Desert Shield was the largest military transport effort ever undertaken by the United States.

This was no exaggeration. Once the movement of people and equipment began, an airplane was arriving in Saudi Arabia every 7 minutes. C-5 Galaxy and C-141B Starlifter crews began pushing the outer limits on the maximum permitted flying time per month—normally 235 hours—and maintenance people began coaxing extra capabilities out of their aircraft. No outfit has higher safety standards—or a better safety record—than Johnson's MAC, and nobody was taking any short cuts, but a maximum effort was under way to get the big airlift ships into the air and keep them moving.

The crews staged out of familiar bases in Europe—Torrejon, Spain; Zaragoza, Spain; Ramstein, Germany; Rhein-Main, Germany. An airlift mission might be launched from anywhere—the job might be, for example, to haul equipment for the 82nd Airborne from Fort Bragg. A crew would be assigned to fly the first leg of the mission—for example, from Fort Bragg (actually, adjacent Pope AFB) to Torrejon. Once our C–141B or C–5 crew arrived in Torrejon, it would find other crews in a pool, waiting. One of these waiting crews would pick up the mission and the aircraft at Torrejon and continue downrange. The crews called this the eastbound stage, and when they arrived downrange they needed to find their way *back* to Europe. This could make for a long day.

Hard work for the key players

On trans-Atlantic flights, up to thirty-six tankers and airlifters, instead of the usual three or four, were seeking clearance from air traffic controllers daily. More were flying downrange—between Europe and the gulf. Problems were bound to occur. An amateur radio buff in England picked up a transmission from a C–141B Starlifter pilot who had a problem with one of his wings. "It's between the fuselage and number 3 engine," the pilot supposedly radioed. "The skin is peeling back." According to another report, a KC–10 tanker had to turn back over the Atlantic after its refueling boom dropped off. Another aircraft suffered the loss of two of its four engines. None of these reports have been verified by official sources and it must be remembered that problems—often less serious than they may sound to the layperson—are inevitable

On the Saudi desert, a pilot of the 1st Tactical Fighter Wing runs up engines on F–15C Eagle 83–0026, wearing the red fin color of the wing's 71st Tactical Fighter Squadron. On the first day of Desert Shield, these fighters departed the East Coast and pilots spent up to 16 hours in their cockpits, refueling six times in the longest overseas deployment ever made by American fighters. Robert F. Dorr

An F–15C fighter taxies out in Saudi Arabia. Robert F. Dorr

A long day for airplane 453

It was the biggest airlift in history. "In comparison, the Berlin Airlift was a picnic," said Airlift Control Element Captain Christopher Mardis, standing on the ground in Saudi Arabia, as giant C-5 Galaxy transports taxied by. "We've moved the equivalent of a big city from one end of the earth to the other. I'm proud to be a part of this. A lesser group of people could not have achieved what we've done here."

But not everything went perfectly. In mid-September 1990, Major L. W. Crane wrote in the "gripe sheet" for C-5A Galaxy 70-0453 that the aircraft had mechanical problems needing attention. Taken together, these problems made airplane 453, in Crane's words, "unsafe for night flying." Another Galaxy pilot also wrote up gripes about 453. In any fleet, one aircraft was always more trouble-prone than others, and in Desert Shield this honor fell to 453.

By October 12, 1990, recurring problems with 453 had not been fixed. A new crew was to take the aircraft from Torrejon on the 9 hour trip downrange. Departure was scheduled for 2:00 p.m.

But 453 had not been fueled or cleaned. Torrejon was busy, with airlifters coming and going, and the pilot could not get help on the busy flight line. Excreta was smeared over the latrine in the C-5A; this was not something the pilot wanted to carry to the heat of the desert.

It took 6 hours for the crew to get these departure problems solved. It was 8:00 p.m. by the time 453 lifted into the air from Torrejon's runway 25.

During the flight to the gulf, the pilot's altimeter went on the blink. An engine problem occurred and was quickly resolved.

The crew had been working for more than 15 hours when the pilot descended for landing at a base in Saudi Arabia. Only then, the pilot learned that the nose wheel would not come down.

It took an extra hour for a loadmaster to crawl down into the nose, lower the nose wheel by hand and ascertain that it was locked into place. The loadmaster heaved a sigh of relief. They could now land.

But they couldn't. Now, the pilot was told that his Saudi destination was fogged in! It would be necessary for 453's crew to divert to another location in the gulf region until the fog lifted.

At the unscheduled divert location, no one greeted the crew. No coffee was available.

The divert added 4 hours to the crew's working day. By the time the fog lifted, enabling 453 to take off again and proceed to its original Saudi destination, the crew had been in the air not for 9 hours, as planned, but for nearly 24 hours.

So big was the airlift, so busy the Saudi airfield, that 453's crew had no opportunity to rest at its scheduled destination. "If we stopped downrange we'd have to stay inside the airplane," said the pilot, "and that's not really rest at all."

There was no choice. The weary crew would have to take the C-5A Galaxy back to Torrejon. At least, thank heaven, Operations told the crew it had no passengers to worry about.

Wrong. It was a mix-up. In fact, 453 did have passengers to Torrejon. Its crew would have to carry them.

For loadmaster Master Sergeant Art McGee, this was the last straw. In Operations, McGee threw his gloves across the room, turned and rammed a fist through a door. Even the heroes of this great airlift were not always at their best. The crew still had not officially passed the limit for safe flying—the 6 hours spent on the ground at Torrejon before getting under way did not count—but this was one crew where exhaustion had taken hold and tempers were on edge.

For the passengers, it was no fun making the 9 hour flight back to Torrejon with an angry crew and no coffee, no amenities and no reason to believe the nose wheel would come down. The hours dragged. The pilot's altimeter went bonko again.

This time, at least, the nose wheel worked; airplane 70-0453 landed at Torrejon, its crew having been on duty for 33 hours. This time, the gripe sheet got attention. This time, 453 was thrown into major overhaul for a thorough fix before flying again.

in an airlift as massive as the one General Johnson's MAC people were pulling off.

Johnson had a number of arrows in his quiver when it came time to make this complicated, difficult airlift do its job. For one, he used his authority as Transportation Command chief to activate stage 1 of the Civil Reserve Air Fleet (CRAF). Stage 1 called for seventeen commercial passenger planes and twenty-one commercial cargo planes to be used for lift activities. This plan had been on the books for years but had never been used before. Stage 2, which could be implemented only by Defense Secretary Dick Cheney, called for 187 commercial passenger and cargo aircraft to be pressed into service. Stage 3, to be implemented in a time of national emergency, called for 506 commercial aircraft to be used. Johnson explained that it was unlikely the second or third stages would have to be implemented.

But Johnson's airlift people faced a formidable challenge. To quote the general, "You don't just fly a lot of airplanes to different places, ask people to fill them up and take off again to carry them overseas." Clear-cut plans had to be made on how to move a unit, how to establish people and equipment at the other end. If, for example, you were moving the Air Force's 363rd Tactical Fighter Wing at Shaw AFB, South Carolina, exactly how did you do it? Did you move first the people who would provide security, or those who would provide food? Did your huge transport planes take off first with portable buildings and furniture for creature comfort, or with supplies of missiles and ammunition to be carried by the 363rd's F-16 Fighting Falcons? Did you deploy the fighters before their maintenance people, mechanics and crew chiefs? An F-16, with air refueling, could be moved to the gulf fairly quickly, but did you want the fighter to arrive before its support people and equipment could get there?

Technical Sergeant David A. Hinojosa is a loadmaster with the 433rd Military Airlift Wing at Kelly Field, a reserve unit called to active duty on the day it lost a crew. The black band across the squadron patch on Hinojosa's right shoulder is a symbol of mourning for the C-5A Galaxy crew headed up by Major John Gordon, which was lost in a crash at Ramstein on August 29, 1990. Robert F. Dorr

Major Stephanie A. Wells was the aircraft commander of a C-5B Galaxy during an airlift flight from Torrejon to an American air base in Saudi Arabia. Wells was one of two officers from the Houston area who visited Judy Gordon to notify her of the death of her husband, John. Robert F. Dorr

Many of these questions cannot be answered because the Pentagon does not want to tell all it knows. With years of practice, problems still arise. At Shaw, beginning August 8, 1990, while F-16s were howling aloft and F-16 support people were scrambling to load up huge C-5 Galaxy cargo planes, the airlifters were arriving faster than the "customers"—the F-16 outfit—could load them. Lessons were learned at Shaw, where temporary logjams slowed the deployment, and these lessons were applied in later movements.

ALCE units

General Johnson's secret weapon was the Airlift Control Element (ALCE, pronounced al-see), a team of experts who set up shop at both ends of the air bridge, putting talent to work optimizing departures and arrivals. These nerve centers took over responsibility for the transport aircraft after landing and oversaw their unloading, reloading and mechanical needs. In many cases, the officers who headed up ALCE units were C-5 or C-141 pilots themselves and could advise Air Force, Army and Marine people how best to organize. The ALCE people knew that the hardest part of any war is moving fighting forces into the field and supplying their gargantuan needs. At the Saudi end, where Captain Christopher Mardis and others of the 438th ALCE unit labored with huge aircraft being "thrown at us at a horrendous rate," the job was critical—and it went well.

Johnson's Military Airlift Command committed ninety-four percent of its mammoth C-5 transports (eighty-nine planes) and eighty-nine percent of its C-141B Starlifters (195 planes) to Desert Shield. All eight of the Navy's fast transports were activated to carry the heavy armor of the 24th Infantry Division (Mechanized) from Fort Stewart, Georgia, whereas other heavy equipment had to travel on slower ships. Sealift had long been neglected when defense dollars were spent, and although more aircraft would have been helpful, more ships were almost essential. Soldiers and marines who made the long ocean voyage to the Persian Gulf took longer than anybody was comfortable with, because there were too few vessels and too many customers.

Nor was the airlift story always one of a big, happy family working together. Tom Loftus found that on one C-141B Starlifter flight to Saudi Arabia, he was in the air for more than 14 hours, of which 8 were spent flying, the remainder spelling another crew. Loftus' weary crew had to struggle with ground personnel who tried to load too much cargo, command posts confused about his destination and a 3 hour quest for an empty bed at the end of one 24 hour mission. Crew fatigue was a round-the-clock problem. These difficulties lent themselves to exaggeration in the telling, and Loftus was among many wanting to make the point that the unprecedented airlift went remarkably well. "I saw dedication of a kind I've never witnessed before," he commented.

While the pace of air and sea transport grew, General John Chain's KC-10 and KC-135 tankers from nearly every Strategic Air Command base were refueling aircraft flying to the Persian Gulf. By August 19, 1990, KC-135s had

Seen through the windshield of a C-5B Galaxy, a Saudi city is lit up in the middle of the night. Robert F. Dorr

flown about 250 refueling sorties and KC-10s more than 100. Among aircraft being refueled were F-117A stealth fighters of the 37th Tactical Fighter Wing, which began their journey to the Mideast by flying from Tonopah Test Range, Nevada, to Langley AFB, Virginia, on August 19.

In those distant deserts so far from home, people and weaponry began arriving from all directions, at all hours. Colonel John McBroom's 1st Tactical Fighter Wing, with its F-15 Eagles, was first on the ground after an exhausting journey that covered 6,500 miles (10,460 kilometers) over 14 hours and required seven midair refuelings and 85,000 pounds (38,555 kilograms) of fuel for each fighter. Air Force officers acknowledged that some pilots spent up to 17 hours in their fighter making the crossing—sore, cramped, with no one to talk to and no way to scratch that persistent itch. On the ground, pitted against Iraq's 600 plane air force, McBroom's F-15 pilots immediately began flying patrol missions—ready to take command of the air if fighting erupted during the vulnerable early days when the US presence in the gulf was still meager and growing.

Close behind came F-15E Strike Eagles of the 336th Tactical Fighter Squadron, part of the 4th Tactical Fighter Wing, deploying from Seymour Johnson AFB, North Carolina. The two-seat F-15E was equipped with Low-Altitude Navigation and Targeting Infra-Red for Night (LANTIRN) pods, conformal fuel tanks, high-resolution radar for ground mapping and automatic terrain avoidance systems. Whereas McBroom's F-16C Eagles were charged with establishing and maintaining air superiority, the F-15E Strike Eagles would take the offensive to Iraq forces on the ground if necessary.

A report in the *Washington Times* that two Iraqi MiG-23 jet fighters fired on two F-15s inside Saudi airspace with both missiles and cannons was apparently in error, although McBroom acknowledged that his Eagle pilots had locked their weapons radar on Iraqi Mirage F1 fighters during missions near the border with Iraqi-occupied Kuwait.

From Langley, F-117A stealth fighters proceeded onward to a location within striking range of Iraq's forces. The F-117A had been designed not merely to evade radar but also to strike high-value targets with exacting precision in the dead of the night. This hush-hush product of the Lockheed Skunk Works was one of many reasons Americans were well-prepared for desert warfare in the nocturnal hours. Despite experience gained in eight years of warfare with neighboring Iran, Saddam Hussein's forces were not effective in combat during the hours of darkness—a weakness the Americans intended to exploit.

If Eagles, Strike Eagles and F-117A Nighthawks were going to fight, air refueling was going to be essential to success. In addition to refueling the stream of aircraft crossing the Atlantic, pausing in Europe and then heading downrange, SAC had to put tankers into position to support combat operations against Iraq. Numerous movements of tankers took place, one of them uprooting the 41st Air Refueling Squadron's KC-135Rs and shifting them rapidly to an air base in the gulf.

Downrange. The moon shines on a C-5B Galaxy, with a CRAF Pan American aircraft in the background, at a US air base in Saudi Arabia. Robert F. Dorr

One of our dramatis personae who symbolizes all the American service members of the nineties, air refueling boom operator Rick Geffken, showed up for work at Griffiss AFB on Friday, August 17, 1990, to learn that his 41st Squadron was deploying. Geffken was told on Friday that he would be going—then, later in the day, that he would not; he would be one of the few people in the squadron to watch things at home. He unpacked his suitcase, put away his travel kit and showed up for work again on Saturday, August 18, to be told things were changed again. In less than 24 hours, Geffken was aboard a KC-135R, call sign ROMA 44, heading eastward from upstate New York and bound for the gulf.

Distant deployment

Rick Geffken accepted this. It came with the turf. Both he and Stephanie had brothers in the

The C-5 Galaxy was the backbone of the air bridge that carried people and equipment to Desert Shield. The Military Airlift Command was conducting about 300 airlift missions per day at the peak of the US military build-up in the Persian Gulf. C-5s were flying 10.5 hours per day, a remarkable total that barely left sufficient time for routine maintenance, cleaning, fueling and other necessities. Robert F. Dorr

Marine Corps who had already been deployed. Geffken's father, an insurance consultant in Benton, Pennsylvania, had done special forces duty in Vietnam. Whatever he may have been thinking about—Stephanie's pregnancy or his auto body business—Geffken went. In earlier years, when the United States had a citizen army, a boom operator would have been less likely to be married, unlikely to own a business. Some critics wondered if people in the new, professional force were really focused on their jobs. Geffken's boss, Colonel Marc L. Drinkham, deployment commander for the Griffiss tankers, made it clear that as far as he was concerned,

the pros of the nineties were up to the task. "The people we have are the best," Drinkham said.

Geffken's KC-135R landed first at Mildenhall, England, perhaps the busiest air base in the world during the peak of Desert Shield air operations. With the American presence in the gulf growing, there was no need to push the rules that called for 12 hours of crew rest before continuing downrange. Geffken showered, ate, slept. It would be August 22, 1990, when he arrived at the tanker base in the gulf.

Crew rest

Crew rest was to become an issue. At Rhein-Main, another stopover for aircrews heading

The Lockheed C-5B Galaxy was nothing if not impressive. The entire nose section was actually a clam-shell door that could be opened to drive vehicles on and off the giant transport. Joseph D. Herman

47

downrange, a tent city sprang up and the base began providing 1,600 showers in each 24 hour period and housing 210 transients per night. At Zaragoza, C–141B Starlifter pilot Tom Loftus felt at ease and comfortable in his role as a reservist volunteering to carry people and equipment to the gulf but noticed that others around him were pushing themselves hard, raising the question of whether fatigue might slow the airlift. Loftus had made several flights, both on the trans-Atlantic leg and on the downrange trip to Saudi Arabia and other gulf locations, carrying soldiers, marines, generators, trucks, food, ammunition. Everybody seemed to be pacing himself or herself, exercising prudence, but Loftus could not help but wonder: Were some of his fellow pilots and aircrews becoming too exhausted?

Not everyone went to the gulf in the same direction as Geffken and Loftus. A C–5 Galaxy pilot from Dover AFB, found himself circumnavigating the globe to pick up marines at Kaneohe Bay, Hawaii, and carry them to the gulf via stopping points in Asia. On this airlift route, the flights were even longer. Almost always, C–141s and C–5s carried relief crews. Still, one flight crew put in a duty day—if it could be called a day—of 38 hours. John McBroom's fighter pilots had put in a long day once to get where they were going; General Johnson's transport crews and General Chain's tanker people were putting in long days, end to end. Could the hard-working MAC airlifters and SAC tanker crews keep it up? Would the best of the best wear themselves out, when there was no second team to call in?

The airlift was perhaps hardest on MAC's loadmasters, who were always the first to hit the ground on foreign soil when a C–5 or C–141B landed. Matt Davis found himself adjusting to some of it because he'd accumulated plenty of

Army and Air Force personnel work together to download a cargo-configured Humm-Vee.

experience coping with jet lag; "You have to let your body function on its own time," he said. But Davis complained of what crews called the MAC Big Eye. This was the condition when your mind said sleep, your body said get up, you'd finally found a bunk and the eyes just wouldn't close.

Back home, the C-5B Galaxy loadmaster's wife, Kelly, was adjusting to a new world. Davis had handled the finances, handled everything. Now, Kelly had a child to worry about, a broken automobile and a full-time job with a van line company—the last, a surrender to the family's discovery that a military salary just wasn't enough. Now, the car, which had gone on the blink at the outset of Desert Shield, was repaired by Kelly, with moral support from nine-month-old son, Brian.

Davis could be gone seventeen days at a time on his airlift missions, and might be weary when he dragged in, but "there'd be no sympathy from *her*," he said. "She'd hand me the list of things that needed to be done around the house." The difficult trips and hardship did not prevent Davis from feeling Desert Shield was all worthwhile. "We can affect the outcome for our country," he said. Often, this meant dealing with poor communication, frustration and mix-ups when loading and unloading cargo under unspeakably difficult circumstances—and under high pressure.

Returning from a trip downrange, Major John M. Gordon, the reservist from Kelly Field who'd volunteered to fly C-5A Galaxy airlift missions, had little time to develop his tennis elbow, to unleash his keen sense of humor or even to puff upon his cigarettes. Gordon was known to his friends as a man who never complained about the costs or sacrifices of being in the reserves, and he was fully qualified as a C-5A aircraft commander. During the back-and-forth scurrying by the huge airlift transports, he completed the latest leg of his latest mission with a routine landing at Ramstein. He phoned his wife, Judy, took care of the billeting needs of his crew and settled in for the requisite crew rest. Like most in the volunteer force of the nineties, Gordon had no problem with ideas that civilians in the outside world regarded as old-fashioned,

even corny. Gordon was a *patriot*, to use a word chosen by his Houston neighbor Joe Kamalick after Gordon's own opinion could no longer be consulted—and although he would never have glorified himself, the major would not have been uncomfortable with the word.

Crew rest. On August 23, 1990, MAC chief General Hansford Johnson said that officials were becoming concerned about the safety of people who had been "sprinting" since the airlift began.

Boom operator Rick Geffken, aboard a KC-135R, arrived in the Persian Gulf area on August 22 in what his outfit called a bare-base deployment—just the essentials, please, in an environment that was not really ready for an SAC tanker squadron. A Prime Beef team (SAC's name for the civil engineers who set up a base and make it work—firefighters, carpenters, plumbers) had arrived just ahead of Geffken, along with the all-essential Air Force security police who had a key antiterrorist role.

Geffken had gotten to the war, as some were now calling it, very early—early enough to see tents going up, air conditioning units installed, equipment unloaded. At his desert location,

The Lockheed C–130H Hercules was the standard tactical "trash hauler" at the outset of Desert Shield. Two Air Force wings were equipped with Hercules transports modified for low-level flying under combat conditions, though these looked just like any other Hercules from the outside. Joseph D. Herman

49

which he cannot name, two KC–135 crews of four people each occupied each tent while the tankers themselves basked in a 120 degree Fahrenheit [49 degree Celsius] furnace. Some of the tankers had been camouflaged in a charcoal-gray color long before Desert Shield and were now 30 degrees Fahrenheit [12 degrees Celsius] or more hotter on the inside than gray-painted tankers.

Geffken and others, working in shorts, T-shirts and combat boots, assembled the new home of the 41st Air Refueling Squadron. Yankee ingenuity helped. With no plan, no blueprints, only the germ of an idea, Geffken and his buddies worked out a way to make refrigerators using wooden boxes, padding them with Styrofoam lining and connecting an air conditioner blower. During breaks, they had time for lizard races ("quick little buggers"), swapping of the few newspapers in circulation and an occasional hand of poker. The men and women of the 41st ate MREs, those plastic-sealed rations known as Meals, Ready to Eat, until a chow hall could be put up. The MREs are, in fact, quite tasty, but no commander could prevent American troops from joking that the acronym meant Meals Rejected by Ethiopia. The chow got better and news of the outside world came from tanker crews that were coming and going.

At this rapidly growing location, public affairs expert Technical Sergeant Jane Blaney arrived on a KC–135R Stratotanker to find that her typewriter had broken in transit. Blaney's job of dealing with the press became moot: the press was still not allowed to visit the new base and the soldiers and airmen were ordered to keep their location secret. Blaney set up her "office" in the back of a shuttle bus for five days, then moved into a tent with no air conditioning. Eventually, she had a tent with cool air but, still,

On the eve of Operation Desert Shield, the Military Airlift Command's fleet of 265 Lockheed C–141B Starlifters was growing old. The C–141B had served since the early Vietnam era, racking up a formidable record of airlift achievements with little notice. Lockheed

no typewriter. "My time is divided between rumor control and the women's latrine-cleaning detail," she wrote home, using ball-point rather than keyboard. In due course, Blaney and other PR workers devised a locally produced newspaper for troops in the field, one of many tools to increase morale and quash rumors.

Rick Geffken, Jane Blaney and the others at this desert location were among the growing thousands of Americans who had deployed to the gulf with a finely honed fighting edge, ready to beat the pants off Saddam Hussein, and found themselves confronting an enemy far more formidable than Iraq—boredom. In those days of late August 1990 when Desert Shield was at its peak but was fast losing its dominance in TV news reports, Americans in the desert were finding that, after setting up shop, they had little to do. You did not pick yourself up from a tent in the desert and go out for a pizza, a beer and a movie. About all you had to look forward to was mail from home. And in late August, suddenly, because the number of Americans deployed had risen so sharply, delays occurred in getting the mail through.

On August 29, C-5A Galaxy 68-0228, belonging to Bill Begert's 60th Military Airlift Wing at Travis AFB but crewed by reservists from Kelly Field, began rolling out on the taxiway at Ramstein for another of the hundreds of airlift missions now being flown around the clock. General Johnson's MAC experts had some concern about the C-141B Starlifter; the aging transports were rapidly approaching their airframes' structural fatigue life. Fortunately the twenty-year-old C-5A, as well as the much newer C-5B Galaxy, was considered to have nearly unlimited fatigue life on its engines and airframe. Nor was fatigue a problem for the crew, it seemed, since it had had a 24 hour layover during this stop at Ramstein.

Carrying medical equipment and other supplies, as well as a normal load of 180,000 pounds (81,646 kilograms) of jet fuel, the C-5A Galaxy was scheduled for a stop at Rhein-Main, home of the burgeoning tent city, to be followed by a trip downrange to an undisclosed Desert Shield location. The Rhein-Main stop may have

been added as a last-minute afterthought. Cleared to turn onto Ramstein's main runway, the C-5A Galaxy received clearance, started its takeoff run, built up speed and began to rotate— aiming its nose at the sky, in position to climb aloft. At the controls was a well-rested, thoroughly skilled Major John M. Gordon.

We may never know what went wrong. Instead of climbing, the C-5A continued rotating until it was in motion at an impossible angle, dragging its tail, still gaining speed. There was a screeching, an explosion. The whole area lit up from burning fuel. The fiery crash of the C-5A at runway's end at Ramstein—just 6 miles (9.65 kilometers) from the Army's Miesau munitions depot, where nerve gas was being stored—killed thirteen airmen, traumatized four survivors, and spoiled the perfect record of the thousands of people and hundreds of aircraft mounting the airlift.

Among the dead was Major John M. Gordon, volunteer reservist. It is unclear whether Gordon ever knew that on the day he died, his reserve squadron was called to active duty. Gordon had not needed to wait until anyone called him. In the civilian world that hired its armed forces because it did not want its sons drafted, John Gordon was a patriot.

For many years, it had been understood in military circles that any surge of activity in response to a crisis would place heavy demands on the United States' reserve forces. This, too, was one consequence of purchasing a professional force to replace a citizen army. Once belittled as "weekend warriors," reserve and National Guard people were, in fact, dedicated professionals. It was common for reservists to outperform members of the regular armed forces in realistic war exercises such as MAC's Airlift Rodeo competition or Tactical Air Command's Gunsmoke air-to-ground contest. Reserve airplanes were often better maintained, babied, spit shined—in short, better looking and better fighting—than those of the regular forces. The reliance upon the reserves, depending on how you looked at it, was a pivotal strength or a glaring weakness in the American ability to fight and win a modern war. It all depended on whether reservists had really meant it when they signed the dotted line. Did they mean it, not just as an abstract notion but deep in their hearts, when they signed up knowing that in a crisis they might be called to active duty? In more than two decades, none had been called up.

On August 29, 1990, Defense Secretary Dick Cheney wrote *his* signature and the Pentagon began calling to active duty 49,703 people from selected reserve and National Guard units to go to the Middle East or to US bases as support personnel for Operational Desert Shield. Many were airlift crews, among them John Gordon, Tom Loftus and others who had already begun "the war" *before* being called up. The call-up affected 24,734 Army, 6,243 Navy, 14,476 Air Force and 1,250 Coast Guard reserve men and women. It took place during the same week Cheney announced that the number of Americans in Saudi Arabia had reached 100,000. Saddam Hussein began to realize that Desert Shield was serious.

If the airlift was the heroic story in Desert Shield, it could not be overlooked that the United States had to ponder an air war against Iraq. The F-15s, F-16s, F-111s, and carrier-based F-14s, F-18s and A-6s were not there for show. If the United States knew how to do one thing, it was to mount a sudden, massive aerial campaign against a well-entrenched opponent. Iraq had some tricks to throw into the equation, including turning off air defense radars to prevent US reconnaissance planes from monitoring the signals, but for every step the United States had a counterstep.

On a September 10 to September 12, 1990, trip to the Mideast, Air Force Chief of Staff General Michael J. Dugan spoke freely of plans to exploit Israeli intelligence data and to mount a massive bombing campaign against Baghdad—specifically targeting Saddam Hussein, his family, even his mistresses. "The cutting edge would be in downtown Baghdad," Dugan stressed, leaving no doubt that the Air Force was not interested in the half-measures it had taken in Vietnam.

By then, the Air Force had 450 combat planes and 250 support aircraft operating from thirty airfields in the gulf and the Navy had three carrier battle groups nearby, and Dugan discussed openly targets they might strike, including Iraqi power systems, missile sites, airfields and rail lines. Some felt Dugan was extolling the virtues of air power without paying enough tribute to the ground forces, which would also have a critical role.

But it was Dugan's candor that rankled his boss. Two days after Dugan's trip to the Mideast, Defense Secretary Dick Cheney relieved him of his job as the United States top airman, saying that he had too readily discussed classified information. It was one of the few signs of discord during Operation Desert Shield. Both Cheney and Dugan were respected and well liked, but Dugan's departure left no doubt who was in charge in the Pentagon. Nevertheless, when no one contradicted the veracity of a word Dugan had spoken, Saddam Hussein may have noticed that the new breed of American military people had passed the test. Says an intelligence expert, "This event scared the pants off of him."

Before Operation Desert Shield began, the American airlift fleet had never been tested under all-out, near war conditions. The Lockheed C–5 Galaxy was the backbone of Military Airlift Command's cargo-hauling armada and was soon to be thrown into the crucible. C–5B Galaxy 84–0061 belonged to the 436th Military Airlift Command at Dover AFB, commanded by Colonel Mike Moffitt, and was displayed at an air show at Chicago O'Hare airport on May 5, 1990. Joseph D. Herman

Chapter 3

Sea

The big question was: can we get our forces in place *before* Saddam Hussein decides to attack? The US Navy's carrier battle groups provided part of the answer.

In the early days of Desert Shield, when only a few Americans were on the ground in Saudi Arabia and these were not yet positioned to do much defending or fighting, military analysts thought they saw a flash point coming. The catalyst was an American request of Egypt's President Hosni Mubarak to allow the aircraft carrier USS *Dwight D. Eisenhower* to transit the Suez Canal in order to be close enough to strike Iraqi targets if conflict should break out. *Eisenhower* would then be able to serve as a watchdog on the Saudi Arabian pipeline terminal at Yanbu, guarding this high-value target. At the same time, USS *Saratoga* (CV-60)—just then departing the United States—would guard the eastern Mediterranean while USS *Independence* prowled the Gulf of Oman. A trio of carrier battle groups, supported by the battleship USS *Wisconsin* (BB-64) and other naval forces, would have the strength to ward off an Iraqi attack and, if necessary, to strike Iraq.

A refusal by Mubarak would shatter the thin veneer of international cooperation painstakingly crafted by the Bush administration in the wake of Iraq's August 2, 1990, invasion of Kuwait.

If Egypt allowed *Ike* to transit, other problems would arise. Would not Saddam Hussein's military staff see this as the time to strike, before

the Americans could get into place with sufficient numbers to handle an attack? Though it would tax their fuel capacity and staying power to the limit, would not Iraq's MiG-23 and Su-22 ground attack aircraft be able to swarm down on *Eisenhower* while she was bottled up in the narrow canal, lacking freedom to maneuver? And if Saddam Hussein learned from *Ike*'s passage that fellow Arabs were joining the stand against him, would he not see even more reason to launch a preemptive strike, before the other side could be better prepared?

Because of the time difference, President George Bush got up at 2:30 in the morning on August 6, 1990, to telephone President Hosni Mubarak. It was part of an orchestrated campaign of personal diplomacy by Bush that included thirty-five personal calls to foreign leaders, gathering up support from numerous capitals for a stand against Iraq.

In fact, support from other nations exceeded what Bush might have hoped for, and even Egypt and Syria sent troops of their own to help in the defense of Saudi Arabia. But the situation was still unfolding when a clear, crisp August 7 dawned and *Eisenhower* began her transit of the Suez Canal. Not much has been said about the transit, but it must be assumed *Ike*'s crew was ready for trouble. Mike Nevatt, the fuel chief on *Ike*, like many of the 5,000 aboard the nuclear-powered carrier, spent most of the time below decks—unable to enjoy the splash of sun against sand all around them—

The aircraft carrier was the capital ship of the all-volunteer US forces on the eve of Desert Shield. USS America *(CV–66), seen here, was in Norfolk, Virginia, and would be available to relieve the carriers already committed when the Persian Gulf build-up began. Already at sea in the region were USS* Independence *and USS* Dwight D. Eisenhower, *soon joined by USS* Saratoga. *As Desert Shield unfolded,* Ike *was relieved by USS* John F. Kennedy. *Robert F. Dorr*

attending to duties. The Pentagon hasn't said so, but it would be a fair guess that some men were on deck with Stinger missiles, thinking seriously about Iraq's MiGs and Sukhois.

The Suez Canal is important because it shortens the water route from the Mediterranean to the Persian Gulf by up to 4,800 miles (7,725 kilometers), compared with the exhausting route around the Cape of Good Hope. It is 105 miles (170 kilometers) long, lies at sea level with no locks throughout its length and has a main channel with more than 100 feet (31 meters) deep with a minimum depth of 35 feet

(10.83 meters). As it turned out, *Ike*'s crew was able to concentrate on pilotage and navigation, free from assault. As it turned out, the carrier's transit was an anticlimax and other vessels too began making the journey, including the French destroyer *Dupleix* (DD-0641), when President Francois Mitterand decided to lend support to the stand in Saudi Arabia.

The aircraft carriers, with their powerful strike forces of F/A-18 Hornets and A-6 Intruders, their F-14 Tomcat fighters and other warplanes, rightly received plenty of publicity while the United States continued its build-up through mid-August 1990, but plenty of other sailors were doing their part, on vessels ranging from the mighty battleship *Wisconsin* to nimble destroyers like the USS *Goldsborough* (DDG-20). To the destroyers fell the task of stalking and boarding ships carrying cargo to Iraq, now that the UN Security Council endorsed an American call for economic sanctions.

The flash point came and went. Long after *Eisenhower* completed her transit, no Iraqi attack had occurred. The value of the aircraft carrier was demonstrated—the way one naval officer saw it, having *Independence* and *Ike* on the scene almost immediately bought time for the Air Force to get set up on the ground. Thereafter, the American build-up reached the point where an attack was no longer an appealing choice for Saddam Hussein.

Sealift mission

Far less glamorous was the job of providing sea transport—a job for glory was in short supply and funding had long been niggardly. Some of the torrents of sweat poured from men and women not on a distant desert but in Navy yards and port facilities where sealift vessels were brought up to readiness.

When the decision was made to land a 45,000 strong Marine Expeditionary Force, the 1st MEF, in Saudi Arabia, two Marine brigades were airlifted and their heavy equipment (including tanks, ammunition and other supplies for thirty days) arrived by means of maritime prepositioning ships—five vessels from Diego Garcia and four from Guam.

The first ships from Diego Garcia, a remote American bastion in the Indian Ocean, began

On the crowded flight deck of an aircraft carrier in the Mediterranean, an F-14 Tomcat fighter moves into position while hard-working crewmen stand clear. As the Navy's fleet defense interceptor, the Tomcat will become responsible for the protection of each carrier battle group deployed in support of Operation Desert Shield. The pilot in the front seat and the radar intercept officer (RIO) in back have equally critical roles in making effective use of the Tomcat's radar, missiles and gun. Robert F. Dorr

When Operation Desert Shield began, the carrier USS Independence *was in the Indian Ocean, in a serendipitous location for quick movement to the Gulf of Oman. A few days later, these red-suited deck ordnance men were rehearsing their craft, loading an inert AGM–88A HARM missile body aboard the Grumman A–6E Intruder attack jet in the background.* JO2 S. W. Bartlett, US Navy

unloading in Saudi Arabia on August 15, 1990. Thus, the marines received immediate supplies of much-needed weapons and equipment. The two Marine brigades flew from two locations, Twenty-nine Palms, California, and Kaneohe Bay, Hawaii. The 4th Marine Expeditionary Brigade at Camp Lejune, North Carolina, a completely self-sustained amphibious force with its own aviation, ground combat, combat support and command elements, left East Coast ports beginning on August 13 aboard thirteen Navy amphibious ships.

While giant C-5 and C-141 cargo planes plied the routes into Saudi Arabia and other gulf locations, ninety-five percent of the armor, heavy equipment, ammunition and fuel for American troops had to go by means of sealift. The Military Sealift Command, in addition to dispatching its nine maritime prepositioning ships, activated the eight fast sealift cargo ships, which were on a 96 hour activation schedule, and ten afloat prepositioning force ships carrying munitions and supplies for the Army, Air Force and a Navy field hospital. To the fast sealift cargo ships fell the task of carrying the Army's 24th Infantry Division (Mechanized) from Savannah, with many of the M1 Abrams main battle tanks that would be sorely needed in any desert conflict.

USS *Saratoga* sailed from the East Coast on August 7 to relieve USS *Dwight D. Eisenhower*, as had been planned before Desert Shield began. *Ike*'s sailors had been extended on a long and demanding cruise and were seriously overdue for relief, which came shortly after *Sara* transited the Suez Canal on August 21. In another move that was intended to bolster the force in the region and had not been planned in advance, USS *John F. Kennedy* (CV-67) and her battle group loaded and departed East Coast ports on August 15 to take station in the eastern Mediterranean to support Desert Shield.

When flight operations are under way, a carrier deck is a hectic—and dangerous—place. Displacing up to 80,000 tons (72 million kilograms), more than a thousand feet (300 meters) long and carrying as many as 5,500 people, an aircraft carrier is the largest object ever built on this planet, and the business of flexing a 100 plane carrier air wing is busy and demanding. *Ike, Sara, Indy* and *Big John* kept their Tomcats, Hornets and Intruders flying around the clock, practicing up, maintaining readiness and patrolling any pathway that might be taken by Iraqi jets seeking to hit the carrier battle groups.

Most of this flying was carried out with a safety record that exceeded the best record of normal peacetime operations. It was not until September 26, 1990, that the carrier force suf-

fered its first mishap: the loss of an SH-3H Sea King helicopter from 7th Antisubmarine Squadron aboard USS *John F. Kennedy*. The chopper lost power in one of its two turboshaft engines and made a forced landing in the Red Sea within sight of *Big John*. Sixteen passengers and four crew members were quickly rescued.

Whereas the news media were taken aboard carriers and treated to steamy catapult launches by Tomcats and mock bomb runs by Intruders, far less attention was paid to the ves-

The moment Desert Shield began, Egypt's President Hosni Mubarak was asked to allow USS Dwight D. Eisenhower to transit the Suez Canal to reach the Red Sea and Persian Gulf area where fighting might erupt. One of Ike's squadrons was the Ghostriders of

VF-142, where pilots like Lieutenant Tim "Eel" Morey flew the Navy's premier fighter, the F-14A+ Super Tomcat. Here, in early August 1990, a Ghostrider A+ flies in the region with a load of Sidewinder, Sparrow and Phoenix missiles. US Navy

The second carrier to reach the Desert Shield region was the nuclear-powered USS Dwight D. Eisenhower, which transited the Suez Canal on August 7, 1990. Navy planners did not want carriers inside the Persian Gulf, which they considered too narrow and shallow for the maneuvering necessary to avoid becoming a tempting target. Ike operated in the Red Sea and USS Independence prowled the Gulf of Oman, entering the Persian Gulf only briefly to demonstrate that it could be done. US Navy

Desert Duck was an SH–3H Sea king antisubmarine helicopter aboard USS Independence at the outset of Desert Shield naval activity. An Indy crew member is checking the helicopter's flex-type main landing gear in mid-August 1990. US Navy/JO2 S. W. Bartlett

The Persian Gulf region was not new to the US armed forces. In the late eighties, "reflagging" and naval escort guaranteed the safety of oil tankers threatened by Iran, which belonged to none other than Kuwait. In this October 21, 1987, view, the guided missile frigate USS Hawes (FFG–43) leads a Kuwaiti tanker through the gulf, with help from an SH–60B Sea Hawk helicopter and the guided missile cruiser USS Standley (CG–32). US Navy

Grumman A–6E Intruder 162199, tail hook lowered, settles in for a landing aboard USS John F. Kennedy *during exercises in the weeks immediately preceding Desert Shield.* Big John *is one of the few carriers in the fleet still to be equipped with Vought A–7E Corsairs, one of which is visible in the background together with the requisite brace of Tomcats. Ricky Rizzo*

sels at sea carrying marines who would have to storm ashore in occupied Kuwait if a conflict ensued. To be sure, the marines on the desert— drawing a line just south of the Kuwait border— received some coverage as they humped around the dunes, but those who remained on board ship endured equally harsh conditions as they waited . . . and waited.

Reserve call-ups

Another flash point, though a less likely one, came on August 18, 1990. Two Navy frigates, USS *Reid* (FFG–30) and USS *Robert G. Bradley* (FFG–49), intercepted Iraqi tankers and fired warning shots. The warships kept the tankers

Critical to Marine Corps plans for fighting in the Middle East was the AV–8B Harrier II ground attack aircraft, capable of short takeoff and landing opera- *tions from the decks of warships and from ground locations in the combat zone. McDonnell Douglas*

under surveillance, ready to board them if necessary to enforce economic sanctions. It was the first of numerous encounters on the high seas, and it passed without violence.

Around the United States, suitcases were packed, kisses exchanged and yellow ribbons hung as more and more Navy people were called to the Persian Gulf. With them went large numbers of Naval Reserve people, called to active duty in several increments.

For the first time since World War II, Coast Guard reserves were called to active duty. What had once seemed an arcane specialty—protecting ports for arriving troops and equipment—had become a hot-ticket item on the military's "needs" list. The 303rd Port Security Unit

Navy men are alert on the bridge of the USS John F. Kennedy *as the carrier works up off the Atlantic coast immediately before heading for the Middle East. The captain of the vessel has his own spot on the bridge (not shown) but these men are the key players in moving the 70,000 ton (63 million kilogram) vessel while warplanes take off from and land on its deck.* Ricky Rizzo

During workups just before heading eastward for Desert Shield, an A–6E Intruder recovers on the deck of USS John F. Kennedy. *Deck hands like the arresting gear crew member in foreground, his duties identified by his green shirt color, are critical to successful carrier operations. A few days after this photo was taken,* Big John *embarked for the Middle East, where USS* Dwight D. Eisenhower *was ready to come home.* Ricky Rizzo

For air defense of its carrier battle group, USS Independence *carried two F–14A Tomcat fighter squadrons. This tomcat belongs to VF–154 Black Knights, led by Commander Sel Laughter. The other F–14A squadron aboard the carrier during Desert Shield was VF–21 Freelancers with Commander C. J. "Heater" Heatley as skipper.* US Navy/JO2 S. W. Bartlett

in Milwaukee, Wisconsin, was first to go, uprooted abruptly and flown to the Persian Gulf on September 18. What few people appreciated, even after the call-up, was that the Coast Guard Reserve possessed the nation's only trained port security teams.

The Suez Canal became a familiar sight to American sailors as warships transited between the Mediterranean and the Desert Shield region. On August 22, 1990, the guided missile destroyer USS Tattnall *(DDG–19), a part of the USS* Dwight D. Eisenhower *carrier battle group, proceeds north through the 105 mile (170 kilometer) canal en route to an overdue return to its home port in the United States. US Navy/PH3 Frank A. Marquart*

At the 301st Port Security Unit in Oswego, New York, Richard Ferguson needed no crystal ball to tell him that he and his cohorts would be next. The timing was far from convenient. Ferguson had just given up a thirteen-year career with the Oswego County sheriff's department— the last five years as a helicopter pilot—to work with his father on his campground on Lake Ontario.

More uprootings

Paul Shippers, a machinery technician with the 301st, began packing even before the phone rang. When it did ring, Shippers learned that he and fellow Coast Guard reservists would be going to "an undisclosed Saudi Arabian port." This was more information than many military people were able to share with their families. Some, deployed to other gulf states like Qatar and Oman, were not even permitted to name the

Deck crew members aboard the carrier USS John F. Kennedy *work on F–14A Tomcats belonging to VF–32 Swordsmen, the same squadron that knocked down two Libyan MiG–23s in January 1989. By the end of August 1990, squadron and carrier were in the Persian Gulf region as part of Desert Shield.* Ricky Rizzo

Supporting the Marine expeditionary forces located both at sea and on the ground facing occupied Kuwait, the 17,500 ton (15,750,000 kilogram) ammunition ship USS Suribachi (AE–21) *passes southbound through the Suez Canal en route to the Red Sea on August 8, 1990, at the start of the major American* build-up. *The oldest of 13 ammunition ships now in the Navy, the 512 foot (159 meter)* Suribachi, *completed in 1956, is designed to transfer munitions to other vessels while under way.* US Navy/PH3 Frank A. Marquart

country they'd be in. Leaving behind a nine-year-old son, Shawn, and a sixteen-month-old daughter, Stephanie, Shippers was—like so many—temporarily leaving a better-paying civilian job.

Richard Ferguson got the expected phone call, as did the others, and spent Friday evening pushing uniforms into green duffel bags and saying so long to wife, Diane, daughter Samantha, age three, and sons Christopher, age eight, and Matthew, age six. The campground business, so promising a few days ago, would probably hold

until he got back, Ferguson thought, but how could you tell?

In a tearful farewell at Syracuse's Hancock International Airport, the Coast Guard reservists climbed aboard a C-130 Hercules and departed while F-16 Fighting Falcons from the local Air National Guard base—not part of Desert Shield—taxied past, two pilots giving families the thumbs-up, one offering a salute.

It was not easy, getting to Saudi Arabia. The Syracuse group was flown to Rochester, New

For the members of the sea services, the biggest challenge posed by Desert Shield was the rapid sealift of enormous numbers of military people and weapons to the Mideast. At Savannah, US Navy ships are *ready to take on tanks and armored personnel carriers of the 24th Infantry Division (Mechanized) from nearby Fort Stewart. US Coast Guard/PAl Chuck Kalnback*

The AH–64 Apache tank-killing helicopter was subject to a critical General Accounting Office (GAO) report while Operation Desert Shield was under way, but it performed well in the Persian Gulf region and was accident free from August 1 to October 15, 1990. This Apache is being loaded out at Savannah with the help of Coast Guard port security people. US Coast Guard/PA1 Chuck Kalnback

York, then Toledo, Ohio, where they hooked up with seventy-five guardsmen from units in Buffalo, New York, and Erie, Pennsylvania. They proceeded, then, to Camp Perry National Guard Base near Sandusky, Ohio, for two days of briefing. Among their briefing materials was some of the intercultural tripe the military bureaucracy had begun churning out faster than copying machines could accomodate it:

"Arabs stand very close together when talking," one information sheet told Ferguson. "Stroking the moustache in connection with an oath or promise indicates sincerity. Arabs do not accept or give criticism directly." Much of this was worse than useless since (1) most Americans were not going to talk much with Arabs anyway, and (2) any American was going to be immediately identified as a foreigner from a mile away. Some of it wasn't even right. One coast guardsman wondered how a clean-shaven Saudi, of whom there were many, could show that he was sincere.

The Coast Guard cutter Key Largo escorts the Navy sealift vessel Regulus out of the port of Savannah during the Operation Desert Shield loadout. US Coast Guard/PA1 Chuck Kalnback

From Sandusky, it was a long haul, via a stop in Europe, before the Coast Guard reservists reached the heat and sands of Saudi Arabia. They, at least, had water to go along with the endless expanse of beach. Living accommodations were not available, and again the story was played out—tents, portable air conditioners, portable potties. Ferguson, Shippers and the others threw themselves into the job of guarding the port and unloading fast-arriving sealift vessels filled with the people and machinery of war.

On September 4, 1990, in the Gulf of Oman, crewmen from the guided missile destroyer USS *Goldsborough* boarded the Iraqi-registered merchant ship *Zanoobia*, which was carrying a shipment of tea to Basra, Iraq, and diverted the ship to a nonprohibited port. Key members of the boarding team belonged not to the Navy but to the Coast Guard. Early in Desert Shield, Coast Guard boarding teams had been requested as a result of their proven track record in antismuggling operations. Team members had experience in boarding and searching a variety of merchant vessels, in understanding nautical documents and vessel manifests, and in carrying out general seizure procedures.

To demonstrate that marines at sea in the gulf really were ready to fight, an eighteen-ship, ninety-aircraft amphibious exercise was turned

The sealift that supported Operation Desert Shield set new records for speed, tonnage and just about every other measurement for the unique task of shipping the wherewithal of war from American locations to the Persian Gulf region. This scene shows tracked vehicles arriving by sealift at a port in Saudi Arabia. US Navy

The 24th Infantry Divisions equipment arrives at a Saudi Arabian port. US Army/Gil High via Michael Green

A TOW missile configured Humm-Vee stands ready at a Saudi Arabian port to be shipped downrange. US Army/Gil High via Michael Green

loose in the North Arabian Sea on October 1, 1990. That same day, USS *Independence* entered the Persian Gulf—the first carrier to operate in the gulf's narrow waters in seventeen years—and demonstrated that its Tomcats and Intruders could do the job despite the confines of geography. The landing exercise included a surface and heliborne operation on a remote beach, and air cover included AV-8B Harriers, CH-53 Stallions, AH-1 Cobras and CH-46 Sea Knights.

Carrier operations, amphibious rehearsals and the trailing, boarding and diverting of Iraqi ships were the most visible part of the sea effort during Desert Shield. However, by October, as the American force in the gulf region neared its peak, more than 100,000 sailors, Coast Guard members and marines were at sea against Iraq. Bleak moments occurred—tragedy finally struck

En route to the possible battle zone, the US Navy guided missile destroyer USS Scott (DDG–995) transits southbound through the Suez Canal to the Red Sea on September 24, 1990. Surface warships like the Scott played a major role in enforcing the United Nations economic sanctions that barred cargo-carrying merchant traffic from Iraqi ports. US Navy/PH3 Frank A. Marquart

Previous page
Typical of the US naval forces that practiced in and around the Persian Gulf before Desert Shield came along, these guided missile warships are being led by an SH–60B Sea hawk. US Navy

on October 8 with the loss of two seaborne Marine UH-1N Huey helicopters, 160178 and 160622 of Squadron HMLA-267, taking eight lives—but safety records continued to exceed the best records of normal peacetime operations. The sea services had given Saddam Hussein plenty to think about.

The aircraft carrier USS Dwight D. Eisenhower *transits the Suez Canal northbound on September 24, 1990, following its role in Desert Shield.* US Navy

A gunner's view of the USS Dwight D. Eisenhower *in the Suez Canal. With little space to maneuver, the huge carrier is very vulnerable to attack while in the Canal and vigilance is high.* US Navy

Chapter 4

Land

As with the men and women at sea, the troops on the ground in Desert Shield faced the challenge of getting themselves, their equipment, their weaponry to the right place, fast, before an aggressive Iraq could take advantage of their initial small numbers. The lieutenant colonels who would lead battalions, the lieutenants who would lead platoons and the noncommissioned

officers (NCOs) who made everything work were suddenly thrust into a crisis at a time when all had been charged with doing their job with less. Before the invasion of Kuwait, most had already been scrimping and scrounging. The Pentagon

Air Force security policemen stand guard at a gate to an American air base in eastern Saudi Arabia. Most service people rushed to the gulf region brought a combination of North Atlantic Treaty Organization (NATO) style utilities, worn here, and the lighter-colored garb intended for desert wear. Robert F. Dorr

Secretary of Defense Dick Cheney meets with American troops in Saudi Arabia on August 25, 1990. Second in command behind President George Bush, Cheney was a key participant in the planning and execution of Operation Desert Shield. US Air Force/F. Lee Corkran

had coined a new word—*downsizing*—to describe what it was doing to the armed forces, and those who fought on the ground had been hardest hit.

All the services faced reductions in people, equipment and funding—a result of America's binge over many years, of its families, corporations and government paying their way in life with ever-increasing debt. In August 1990, the biggest problem facing Americans was not Saddam Hussein: it was the budget deficit.

General Carl E. Vuono, the rock-tough Army Chief of Staff, warned his men and women in uniform that budget cuts were going to hurt. Going into the final decade of the twentieth century, the Army would be constricted to its smallest size since the lean years before the Korean War. The Marine Corps' salty commandant, General Al Gray, warned that even those who'd volunteered for the sweat and sacrifice of a military career could not be assured that they'd be

24th's soldiers are transported downrange by bus. US Army/Gil High via Michael Green

Temporary quarters for incoming troops were set up in Saudi Arabian warehouses. This warehouse was *used by the 24th Infantry Division.* US Army/Gil High via Michael Green

kept on board. Cuts were going to be drastic, pay raises were dead as a serious issue, promotions would be slow. On the battlefield, officers were going to have to find a way to fight and win with a little less of everything.

In the two years since becoming the United States' highest-ranking marine, Gray had revived the deep-rooted but often ignored tradition that everyone in the Corps—even a postal clerk or an aviation mechanic—was an infantry soldier first. He had pointedly criticized Pentagon officers who spent their lunch hour jogging along the Potomac in designer shorts, saying that he wanted killers, not athletes. He pressed officers to read a new handbook, *Warfighting*, chock-full of battlefield wisdom from Karl von Clausewitz and Sun-tzu. He changed

the Corps' training syllabus so that every enlisted marine went through a thirty-day, combined-weapons infantry course before boot camp.

Vuono's army, like Gray's marine corps, wanted soldiers who could think as well as fight. American soldiers in combat units such as infantry and armor were routinely given sixteen weeks of basic training at the start of their career, more than ever before. The sergeants, those NCOs who make or break a fighting force, were nearly all sent to the Army's Primary Leadership Development Course, a four-week school for battlefield leaders.

Both the Army and the Marine Corps stressed "maneuver warfare," with fluid movements, quick decisions and bold tactics. A few

24th's soldiers lay platforms for their tents. US Army/Gil High via Michael Green

units, like the 82nd Airborne and Marine expeditionary brigades, were trained to go first, to arrive on short notice and to fight with little. The Army's light infantry outfits were respected around the world and seemed ideal for a post cold war period when the enemy might be a band of Latin drug lords or a Panamanian dictator.

Little of this thinking and planning had been aimed at the kind of confrontation that unfolded in August 1990—against an Iraqi force with modern weaponry and heavy tanks. The Army's Dragon antitank weapon had been derided by the *Washington Post*'s George Wilson as a national disgrace—a line-of-sight weapon that required a soldier to remain in place, guiding the warhead, after its exhaust flash had given away his location. The AH-64 Apache antitank helicopter, praised by those who fly it, had been panned as a technical nightmare by a General Accounting Office report that found the Apache to have serious reliability problems. The M1A1 Abrams main battle tank with its 120 millimeter gun was unquestionably the finest hunk of fighting armor in the world, but nearly all M1A1s were in Europe, and forces slated for Mideast duty were equipped with the older M1 with a 105 millimeter gun and even the M60A1 from the early sixties. All these criticisms are exaggerated, but it remained true that many US weapons had yet to be tested in a modern conflict.

Strong challenge

If Americans in uniform were to stand against Saddam Hussein's 5,500 main battle tanks—to defend Saudi Arabia, to reinforce operation Desert Shield's Four Points or per-

The 24th Infantry Divisions tent city. US Army/Gil High via Michael Green

The 24th's tent city is guarded by a troop-carrier configured Humm-Vee. US Army/Gil High via Michael Green

The standard Army combat vehicle, the Humm-Vee, or Hummer, was manufactured 6 inches too wide to be double-rowed in the Air Force's large cargo planes. Flexible and suitable for action in the desert, the Hummer, like any item of equipment, had to be used *properly. Some examples arrived in the desert with too much air in the tires. These suffered tire explosions before troops realized that tire pressure had to be reduced in the hot climate.* Joseph D. Herman

haps, as some contemplated, even to attack Iraq itself—were the people and their equipment up to the job?

The all-volunteer Army and Marine Corps had little in common with the citizen militia that had protected American interests until 1975. To a Rip Van Winkle, awakening after a slumber of many years, the force would have been unrecognizable. Of 351 military occupational specialties, 302 were open to women. In the top NCO ranks, thirty percent of the Army's sergeant majors and 17.5 percent of the Marine Corps' were black. The Army and Marine Corps had in their ranks the highest percentage of married people, the highest number of people married to each other, the most single parents in military history.

In an earlier time, soldiers and marines spent their waking hours training or working,

Familiar American items of equipment suddenly acquired a new look as Desert Shield caused them to be painted in desert camouflage, some for the first time. One such item was the Humm-Vee, the nineties' version of both the 4x4 truck and the familiar Jeep.

Fifteen feet (4.64 meters) in length, with a curb weight of 5,200 pounds (2,358 kilograms), the Humm-Vee routinely carries a .50 caliber (12.7 millimeter) machine gun, as shown. LTV

The M1 Abrams tank with its desert-sand camouflage and 105 millimeter gun, as shown, was the principal land battle weapon of US Army forces in the Persian Gulf region, whereas some Marine Corps units were equipped with older M60A1 tanks. Two months after the start of Desert Shield, the newer M1A1 Abrams with 120 millimeter gun still had not been shipped to the gulf region. US Army

An M60 tank in the Saudi desert. US Army

82nd Airborne M551 Sheridan tanks. US Army

lived together in barracks, ate together in the mess hall and used their meager pay for 25 cent movies on post or for carousing together, sometimes in red-light districts, on Saturday night. The NCOs and officers remained in the same unit for a prolonged time, getting to know their soldiers, forging a leadership role through patience and diligence.

In the nineties, married soldiers and marines were more likely to live at home and eat their meals at home. The NCOs and officers were on board for shorter periods, with fewer opportunities to strengthen the bonds so needed in a fighting unit—and distracted by graduate courses in management, which seemed more important to a career than killing the enemy on the battlefield. Even in General Al Gray's lean, green machine, the 195,000 person Marine Corps, the buzz word *management* often came up when promotions were sorted out. Gray himself was gruff, abrupt and impatient, and ofttimes went against the grain by saying it didn't matter if you could manage, what mattered was to beat the pants off the bad guys.

Some, who made their living as "military analysts"—those talking heads of cable news and bylines on the editorial page—questioned whether the all-volunteer infantry of the nineties was too pampered, its people too distracted by children, by college courses, even by outside businesses. Most of these analysts were too old to stop a tank with a Dragon or anything else and had served in a different army that was mostly single, mostly white and mostly draftee. It scarcely mattered whether they had a point: George Bush, Dick Cheney, Carl Vuono, Al Gray and H. Norman Schwarzkopf were not in a position to choose what kind of force they would place in Saddam Hussein's tracks. The American people had made that decision.

Cut from the same cloth as the Marines' Al Gray, a weight lifter throughout his years at West Point, General H. Norman Schwarzkopf—the commander downrange—was gruff, solid, uncharismatic, more comfortable with combat troops than with management seminars. Schwarzkopf didn't mind being called the Bear but had never encouraged anyone to call

him Stormin' Norman or, because of the butts he smoked, H. Norman Cigar. The Commander in Chief of US Central Command, in charge of all soldiers, sailors and airmen in the Persian Gulf region, Schwarzkopf was also the right kind of leader for the nineties: he would tell subordinate commanders what he wanted to accomplish and give them considerable latitude to find a way.

Americans who faced imminent combat, and those who watched at home on TV screens, adjusted once again to the discomfort of a "war"—it was not yet a war, but it could be, any instant—utterly lacking in understandable front lines. In Vietnam, the front lines simply hadn't existed: the enemy swarmed inside and among American forces. In Saudi Arabia, the lines were there, and indeed President George Bush had been accurate in "drawing a line in the sand"—but the American media agreed to voluntary restraints that had never before been asked in their history. They agreed not to name specific locations of US forces or to disclose their size and capabilities.

Lines in the sand

Within the constraint on disclosure, the media could say that American troops started out by drawing up a second line of defense, positioning themselves behind a thin line of Saudi troops, who, in turn, were also located some miles back from the Iraqi and Kuwaiti forces. US Marine expeditionary troops arrayed themselves to the extreme east of Saudi Arabia, facing occupied Kuwait, just behind a row of Saudi forces so thin as to be of marginal consequence at best. Other marines remained part of amphibious forces at sea. US Army troops, spearheaded by the lightly armed 82nd Airborne Division, which soon had plenty of company, drew up their battle lines slightly to the west. The men and women of the 82nd had been prepared to parachute into Saudi Arabia under combat conditions—and, indeed, they might yet parachute into Baghdad—but in the beginning, at least, an airdrop was not part of the story. H. Norman Schwarzkopf and other commanders set up their forces to make maximum use of air

A new sight on Saudi sands was the M270 launcher for the US Army's Multiple Launch Rocket System (MLRS), a self-propelled unit firing a free flight artillery rocket designed to fill a void in conventional artillery support. The MLRS was designed to suppress enemy air defense missiles and guns and to bring counterfire to bear on enemy ground positions. LTV

cover and night-vision capabilities, and to allow flexibility of movement in the face of what could be a large-scale assault by Iraqi main battle tanks.

As Desert Shield got under way, the first troops to go in—the 82nd and 101st Airborne, and the Marines—had to be ready for the worst in case Saddam Hussein got antsy before a significant force had arrived in place. The problem went almost unnoticed, but in mid-August 1990, with the first troops stepping off C-141s and the bulk still packing up to go by sea, the few Americans on the scene were exceedingly vulnerable.

American soldiers and marines quickly increased their number behind Saudi troops who made up a thin, brittle line facing the frontier

When the 82nd Airborne Division sent paratroopers to the Persian Gulf region, it also deployed its aviation brigade, equipped with UH–60 Black Hawk and AH–64A Apache helicopters. The Apache is the army's tank killer, the ideal antidote to Iraq's vast force of main battle tanks. Robert F. Dorr

With the knowledge that Saddam Hussein's forces possessed chemical weapons—and had used them— every American service member in the Persian Gulf was provided with chemical warfare mask and equipment, and required to keep it close at hand. The M551 Sheridan tank under the netting in the background is a tip-off that these mask wearers are members of the 82nd Airborne Division. US Army

87

with Iraq and Iraqi-occupied Kuwait. It was understood that the lightly armed Saudis were doing little more than displaying their flag. An armored punch by Iraq would slice through them like a knife through butter. As they took up positions, the captains and lieutenants in charge of ground-fighting companies and platoons arrayed their people defensively, began rehearsing combat situations and boned up on how to coordinate the efforts of infantry, armor and artillery.

Those first, sweaty days passed. The early arrivals, among them the Air Force's 1st Tactical Fighter Wing and the Army's 82nd Airborne, felt very much alone when they formed an equally thin, largely symbolic, line waiting for a little help from their friends. In those early days, a massed armor attack by Iraq would have been difficult to stop. The highly exposed early arrivals—and Schwarzkopf—held their breath and wondered if Hussein would strike while their necks were out.

Throughout August, the defense force grew and first steps were taken to create an offensive capability. Saddam Hussein's "window of opportunity" began to close as the strength of the American commitment deepened.

An example of flexibility, and of strong commitment to mobile action, was a Marine light armored infantry scout unit that introduced the previously untested 60,000 pound (27,215 kilogram) M2 Bradley fighting vehicle.

A 101st Airborne soldier prepares to load an Apache's 30 mm chain gun. US Army/Gil High via Michael Green

101st Airborne soldiers load Hellfire missiles on an AH–64 Apache. US Army/Gil High via Michael Green

These Marine scouts began rehearsing rapid movement on the desert, ready to take out the advance guard of elite forces that would come at the apex of any Iraqi drive. A captain in the unit commented, "We're keeping our edge, we're not going to let things get boring here." The Bradley's M242 Bushmaster automatic stabilized twenty-five millimeter cannon was not powerful enough to confront Iraqi main battle tanks but was an ideal weapon to take out troop carrier and reconnaissance vehicles. Both the M2 Infantry Fighting Vehicle (IFV) and M3 Cavalry Fighting Vehicle (CFV) versions had a two-man turret mounting the Bushmaster gun, supported by the TOW antitank missile system and 7.62 mil-

limeter coaxial machine gun. Early on, before they were authorized live-fire practice, these Marine scouts were rehearsing rapid maneuver and night tactics in the desert. By October 1990, they were joined by the only foreign forces to serve with an American unit, Britain's famed 7th Brigade "Desert Rats," who brought with them far heavier striking power in the form of Challenger main battle tanks.

From the beginning, soldiers and marines were a part of the colossal uprooting that made Desert Shield such an enormous undertaking. Around military camps in the small cities and smaller towns of America, women and men packed up to join Stormin' Norman on the

The two-man crew of a 101st Airborne Apache are strapped in and ready for lift-off. US Army/Gil High via Michael Green

An AH–64 Apache lifts off at a base in Saudi Arabia.
US Army/Gil High via Michael Green

Both the Army and the Marine Corps were equipped with the Bell AH-1 Cobra attack helicopter. The Cobra design dated to the Vietnam era. Modern ver- *sions of the AH-1 had been tested in the deserts of the American southwest and were deemed suitable for operations in the Middle East. USMC*

desert. From one military post to another, in houses, in trailer parks, in open-bay barracks, men and women packed themselves up, said good-by and shipped out. At Fort Stewart, Private First Class Michelle Curphey began on August 8, 1990, watching column after column of M1 Abrams tanks stirring up dust en route to roll-on ships at Savannah. An NCO told Curphey that her unit's personal baggage would be picked up that morning and that everybody would ship out that night. After Curphey's B-4 bag was picked up, she was told she wouldn't ship out for several days, but, in the meanwhile, no one could leave the post.

Curphey had no personal articles, not even a toothbrush. She was one of several soldiers gathered up by a sergeant and told to make a last-minute inspection of four Humm-Vee tactical vehicles.

"We finished the inspection an hour ago, Sarge."

"I don't care. Do it again."

Thus began a 48 hour ordeal of "hurry up and wait." Curphey and her fellow soldiers watched others leave, while receiving confusing and contradictory information on when they, too, could go. Eventually, Curphey was given a movement "slot" and was told she would go to Saudi Arabia not by sea but by air. She began the journey aboard a civil charter airliner with a 3:00 a.m. takeoff.

The most difficult period during Desert Shield was early August when temperatures on the Saudi desert soared to 130 degrees Fahrenheit (54 degrees Celsius). In this environment, anything that offered protection from sun and sunburn was considered an acceptable part of the uniform. This member of the Air Force security police has an informal version of head cover in addition to a helmet. US Army

The US Army's standard helicopter on the eve of Operation Desert Shield was the Sikorsky UH-60L Black Hawk. Like most items of American military equipment, the Black Hawk would prove susceptible to damage from wind and sand in the desert. Joseph D. Herman

Tank arrivals

H. Norman Schwarzkopf and others breathed more easily beginning the third week of August 1990, which was also the third week of the crisis, when sand-colored M1 Abrams tanks of the Army's 24th Infantry Division (Mechanized) under Major General Barry McCaffrey began offloading from USS *Bellatrix* (T-AKR-288), the first of eight fast sealift ships to arrive.

Much has been said about the parched, desert conditions where Americans found themselves. Problems existed. Some tank and helicopter engines needed new mesh screens to protect them from the windstorms that brought blasts of gritty sand through the steamy air. It was discovered that the sand on the Saudi desert had a different texture than the sand at Fort Irwin, California, and in Egypt where realistic battle exercises had been held, and that its density at night could deceive night-vision goggles under some conditions. It was found that some items of equipment coagulated into a useless glob during late morning heat. Aggressive efforts were made to produce "fixes" to these problems, and most reports of poor preparedness for desert warfare were exaggerated. In fact, the Americans had confidence in their equipment and felt ready to fight at night—against an Iraqi opponent who was widely viewed as capable only of daytime warfare.

A look at a dictionary tells us that a *desert* is barren or semibarren land, rendered into a sparse moonscape by meager precipitation. Of the three major kinds of desert—hot, midlatitude and cold—the Saudi desert is the most hostile to human beings, cooking beneath a belt of descending, drying air that is the enemy of rainfall or plant growth. Because of the lack of cloud cover, the land surface heats up to a sizzling broil in daytime but cools abruptly at night, causing a rapid change in temperature. Grit, sandstorms, shimmering haze, even mirages are part of this cruel and empty environment where American men and women were deployed to be ready to fight.

The harsh desert environs were very much on the mind of KC-135R tanker crewman Rick Geffken, who began to consider himself as much

a ground pounder as the troopers in Army and Marine uniform. Yes, there were missions to fly. The hot climate had justified the Air Force's reengining program, which had put four 26,000

This scene was repeated again and again between August 1990 and October 1990 as American ground troops took their officers' advice and drank more water than most had ever consumed before. In fact, they drank so much water that they caused some researchers to believe established ideas about the body's need were out of date. More was better, and it meant surprisingly few cases of heat stroke in the desert. US Army

pound (11,793 kilogram) thrust F108-CF-100 (CFM-56) engines in Geffken's tanker; earlier KC-135A tankers with older, water-injected powerplants simply could not take off from a runway of any reasonable length in 120 degree Fahrenheit (49 degree Celsius) temperatures. The KC-135R was one item in the US military arsenal that performed admirably, but Geffken was still spending most of his time in a tent, racing lizards. As would be the case with Chris Fadness in the Airborne and Curphey in the Army, the enemy was long hours, heat and worries about home.

Officers on the Saudi desert had to ask whether soldiers could keep their edge when the military's "hurry up and wait" routine was allowed to replace a sense of urgency. "We're doing a lot of dumb stuff," wrote 82nd Airborne paratrooper Andrew Bernstrom, age nineteen, to his parents in Champlin, Minnesota. "I'm in complete uniform all the time. The helmet is constantly giving me a headache. The chow gives me dysentery. A lot of people are getting a bit edgy. I've been trying hard to keep my cool." Elsewhere, commanders thought up ways to enhance hard work and horseplay to keep the troops alert.

Our 82nd Airborne tank driver, Private First Class Chris Fadness, found that he and his buddies in the desert were not leading an invasion, as they'd hoped. Still, their spirits were high. They were in the only unit in the Army still equipped with the 16 ton (15,000 kilogram) M551 Sheridan light tank, armed with a 152 millimeter gun and machine guns—a fighting vehicle that dated to 1959 and was still the only tank that could be airdropped. The good news about the Sheridan was that it was highly suited for mobile warfare on the desert against light forces, much like the Bradley, and Fadness and his pals took pride in keeping it in tiptop shape. The bad news, if such it was, was that no one in his right mind would go up against one of Iraq's huge, Soviet-made main battle tanks in a Sheridan. The particular Sheridan that Fadness had driven in Panama nine months earlier was no longer available, for the Army had consigned it to a museum!

Fadness sat down on the desert and put pen to paper:

"Our greatest struggle is with boredom. The days are long, the weeks longer. They try to keep us busy but it's all busy work and it just makes us aggravated. Our tanks are in excellent condition because we have basically fixed everything there is to fix."

Fadness continued, "The night time is our free time if we aren't pulling guard duty or a detail. We get volleyball tournaments going, football games, play chess, read, and do laundry. Laundry sucks because there just aren't enough buckets to do it, plus the fact that we are always conserving water so you have to do it at the right time." In a sense, the TV image of the American soldier slugging down long gulps from a plastic water bottle was a fraud. Fadness and his fellow paratroopers kept having to refill the same bottle from the local water supply.

"The food is okay," Fadness went on. "We get about three sodas a day. The big problem is, the quality of the water is pretty bad. Most [of us] get sick quite often. The zillions of flies don't help, either. We all agree, our living conditions are unsanitary."

Although Norman Schwarzkopf and his officers and NCOs knew it, not everyone seemed to remember that the purpose of shock troops was to fight and win wars. No one, it could be argued, remembered what had happened in Beirut. The last time Americans put large numbers of troops on the ground in the Middle East and *didn't* invade anyone—the last time troops were rushed into a crisis to "hurry up and wait"—a terrorist bomb blew up the Marine barracks in Beirut, killing 241 men. That was in October 1983. Paratroopers and marines did a superb job of adjusting to sitting still in the desert—their performance is one of the great stories of Desert Shield—but all remembered that their stock in trade was fighting.

Fight against boredom

Being bored, in a location where Americans had never served before, created the danger that women and men in uniform would feel betrayed.

But it did not happen. Arriving at the principal US air base in Saudi Arabia in mid-August 1990 after the first flush of excitement over Desert Shield had begun to wane, Michelle Curphey of the 24th Infantry Division (Mechanized) joined dozens of fellow soldiers in lining up for chow, lining up to be issued plastic water bottles and lining up to board buses that would take them to their location in the field. "And, yes, we had to line up to use the latrine, too," she said. It was more "hurry up and wait," but spirits were remarkably high. Soldiers jostled and joked with each other. Curphey observed tiptop spirits and a keen fighting edge.

The mechanized infantry took up positions in the desert. Located behind a token "front line" of Saudi troops who would fall back into their midst if an attack came, the soldiers spent the end of August and beginning of September digging in with their Humm-Vees, M25 Bradley fighting vehicles and M1 Abrams main battle tanks. A news report chiding them for an apparent lack of mobility was discounted by Curphey and the other soldiers as unfair. All along, their job had been to set up defenses first, prepare for offensive action only thereafter. Things improved in September when the Saudi government belatedly permitted live-fire exercises and

Jeeps, Humm-Vees and machine guns; American soldiers in desert attire make their way past tropical foliage in Saudi Arabia. US Army

the Bradleys and tanks began exercising with greater movement.

The soldiers on the desert practiced with night-vision goggles (NVGs). The Army suffered helicopter mishaps while getting settled in the desert—none serious—and the press took a hard look at the NVGs. Even in early October when eight marines were lost aboard two UH-1N Huey helicopters while the pilots were wearing NVGs, every analysis of flying hours, local conditions and individual behavior confirmed that the NVGs worked.

Curphey saw surprisingly little boredom. The troops were working harder than ever, getting their equipment in spit-shined condition.

Curphey's own Humm-Vee tactical vehicles were pristine. "Our people here have a sense that this is a crisis," Curphey wrote in early October to a fellow soldier back at Fort Stewart. "They're behaving as if our deployment here is still the very first item in the news, even if it isn't. We hear from many Americans, relatives and strangers, who send expressions of support. We stay at a peak of readiness."

For Rick Geffken came unexpected relief from life in the hot climes. One of his unit's KC-135R tankers, aircraft 57-1508, needed to be taken back to the United States for a periodic overhaul. It was a grueling, 18 hour flight, but it got boom operator Geffken to upstate New York

Arriving soldiers of the 1st Cavalry Division create a line in the sand at a major airfield in Saudi Arabia as they prepare to draw an issue of bottled water and *then to board buses for their eventual destination in the field.* Robert F. Dorr

on September 24, hours before his wife, Stephanie, gave birth to their daughter. Brittany Megan Geffken arrived early, weighed 6.2 pounds and was in excellent health. Geffken had been granted a miraculous interlude.

Other fathers missed births of children while Americans continued to adjust to life on the desert—with surprisingly few problems, even at the beginning in August when the heat could soar to 130 degrees Fahrenheit (54 degrees Celsius) at the hottest time of day. False-horned vipers and seven-banded scorpions were a threat to troops on the desert, and at least two soldiers were bitten by the snakes, one seriously enough to need surgery. But dehydration and heat stroke proved to be relatively minor problems, simply because the troops were prepared.

More serious was diarrhea, which could range from the "traveler's runs" lasting one or two days to a far more serious affliction caused by salmonella or shigella bacteria found in food and water. The military noted that on average, twenty-eight in 1,000 service people were catching gastrointestinal illnesses—mainly diarrhea—whereas heat prostration struck fewer than two in 1,000.

Nineteen-year-old Private First Class Chris Fadness became twenty-year-old Specialist Chris Fadness with a birthday and a promotion in September. His 82nd Airborne troopers—in a different part of the Saudi desert from the men and women of Curphey's mechanized infantry—were also continuing to act as if a crisis existed, but the danger of boredom grew. By October 11, Fadness wrote:

"We have trained on just about everything possible, sometimes three or more times on the same subject. We are getting pretty restless around here. We seem to be getting a little more time off lately, but all we do is sleep, read, and otherwise be very bored. I can see it in their eyes. We have to fight to keep a sharp edge. Trying to get pumped up and motivated is difficult."

The service members on the ground were up to the challenge. Whether manning a Patriot missile site, pushing a tank through the desert or standing at the ready as part of the seaborne amphibious force, they had done a remarkable job. By mid-October, ten weeks into the most remarkable military build-up in American history, the ground forces were ready.

Chapter 5

War?

By mid-October 1990, ten weeks into Operation Desert Shield, officers fretted that American troops were still not being trained realistically for war on the desert. High-tech items of military equipment were melting, blowing up and springing leaks amid the harsh climate and blowing sand. The risk of chemical warfare persisted.

The troops themselves could hardly have done better, and were highly motivated as the force grew and became entrenched. But for military leaders, it remained a time of uncertainty and dark worry.

What a curious mixture it was—uncertainties coupled with boredom. Terrible worries hanging over the heads of men and women who did not have enough to do. There was the immediate threat of a bloody and monstrous conflagration. But there was also the dragged-out, wearing down of the spirit caused by sheer, simple boredom. It was not a good situation.

The airlift—that greatest, ever, of airlifts, which in August and September broke every record for moving people and equipment across vast distances—began to slow down as the American force settled into place and dug in. Yet the job of flying giant cargo planes continued to be an extraordinary challenge.

As far from Desert Shield as you could get, at Travis Air Force Base, California, Colonel William J. "Bill" Begert passed out routine awards to men and women still shuttling back and forth in his outfit's giant C-5s and C-141s. The modest ceremony held in an open hangar was jam-packed, every parking place in Begert's area of the base overflowing. Among those who couldn't come, one of Begert's classmates from the Air Force Academy sent by fax a deepfelt opinion that the airlift was "A towering achievement in the history of our country and our armed forces."

"We've done a good job," nodded the soft-spoken Begert, sharing the message with others around him. "But we have to keep it up. We have to show that we have the staying power."

Fortunately—defying boredom and drudgery—Military Airlift Command crews refused to give up their sense that the airlift was both important and urgent.

Lieutenant Colonel Thomas G. Loftus, airline pilot turned full-time airlifter, was "fragged" (scheduled to fly) for C-141B Starlifter 64-0627. It was needed so badly, it was yanked out of the paint shop in natural metal and yellow primer before the de rigueur camouflage paint could be slapped on. Lacking the usual lizard-green color coating, the aircraft looked naked—an astonishing breach of procedure—but the needs of the airlift allowed no leeway for cosmetics.

Loftus landed a Starlifter at 3:00 a.m. in Saudi Arabia and was relieved to find temperatures cooling. It was now October 12, 1990, and mercury in the Fahrenheit thermometer plunged to 70 (21 degrees Celsius) at night, while remaining below 100 (38 degrees Celsius) at the hottest hour. More important, the ALCE operation, loading and unloading of the mammoth transport planes was humming. "We had come a long way from where we started," says Loftus, "and our guys were conducting themselves as if this was a crisis atmosphere." To be sure, there was some grumbling. Some airmen wondered after nearly three months when *something* would happen—but nobody was slacking.

Kuwait occupation

Things were, of course, far worse for many others in the Middle East, especially citizens of Kuwait.

In Kuwait, in full control of the country they'd invaded, Iraqi soldiers and security personnel combed government and corporate offices, drawing up lists of people who might lead any resistance, and rounding them up. As early

as August 24, 1990, Iraqi troops surrounded foreign embassies in Kuwait city and began to starve them out.

People were rounded up, too. Kuwaitis with junior positions in the government were taken away. Their families were not told where they were. Some, it was thought, were carted away to Iraq, perhaps never to be seen again. Senior officials were beaten, imprisoned, even shot. A shopkeeper who balked at displaying a portrait of Saddam Hussein was shot in front of his wife. After he lay on the floor of his shop, life ebbing from him, soldiers raised their weapons once more and continued pumping bullets into the man, again and again.

In Kuwait and Iraq, thousands of foreigners were held hostage or caught up in hiding. An estimated 100 Americans, called "human

Members of the 1st Cavalry Division band, carrying M16A1 rifles and musical instruments, greet troop- *ers of the division arriving at an American air base in Saudi Arabia on October 12, 1990.* Robert F. Dorr

shields" by the State Department and "guests" by the Iraqis, were being held at strategic and military sites in Iraq. The idea was that the Americans would balk at bombing an installation if they knew fellow citizens were imprisoned there. Some Special Forces units, in fact, went into training to rescue hostages behind the lines—but Pentagon planners had to draw up target sets without considering this heart-wrenching human factor.

"I am suffering in the Iraqi Gulag," wrote one of the few human shields to get a letter out. "We are held in a place like a medium-security prison, with bars on the windows." As many as three dozen Americans were still hiding out from Iraqi troops. "It's very nerve-wracking here," one wrote in a letter smuggled home on October 16. "Troops all over. This is the first time in my life I have been caged up and I don't like it." Things were little better for ten Kuwaiti-Americans uprooted by Kuwait's occupiers, moved to Baghdad, and detained in a hotel. Twenty-seven Americans were left in the US Embassy in Kuwait.

On August 2 when Iraq overran Kuwait, American ambassador W. Nathaniel Howell had been at the end of his tour of duty, ready to go home. Wives and children of Kuwait-based diplomats, under close scrutiny by the Iraqi occupiers, boarded a ramshackle convoy for an arduous trek to freedom, via Baghdad and the Turkish border. There were heart-wrenching

Soldiers of the 1st Cavalry Division line up at an American air base in Saudi Arabia. Robert F. Dorr

delays and difficulties—which climaxed when teenaged sons of two American diplomats were held back at the border by the Iraqis.

In Kuwait, Howell stayed where he was. He was President Bush's appointee in Kuwait, and United States policy held that Kuwait was an independent nation. The risks taken by career diplomats had rarely been so visible since fifty-two Americans were held hostage in Tehran, Iran, for 444 days in 1979-81.

By August 24 when Iraqi troops sealed off his embassy, Howell feared Saddam's troops might plunder embassies as they had businesses and private homes. In some areas of the city, undisciplined Iraqi soldiers went on a rampage, smashing shop windows with rifle butts, looting, maiming. Long after the fighting was over, an occasional gunshot rang out. There were reports of rape.

In what newspapers called the American "Embassy"—actually, a walled-in, partly-wooded compound near the waterfront with administrative buildings, residences *and* the Embassy—Howell and his colleagues watched and waited. A war of nerves began. Iraqi tanks and armored vehicles circled the compound in a menacing show of force. At any time, the Iraqis could break in. But though they'd abandoned all other pretenses of civility, the Iraqis maintained this one. The Embassy was isolated but not overrun.

Howell, his deputy Barbara Bodine, and other staffers learned how to use an electrical generator to supply power, including the power for their satellite-linked telephone to Washington. A few private Americans took refuge in the compound. Howell and his fellow diplomats continued trying to locate and aid other Americans stranded in Kuwait.

Of course, the United States maintained an embassy in Baghdad, too—minus Ambassador April C. Glaspie, who was in Washington advising Secretary of State James Baker. At both locations diplomats were hampered in their efforts to help fellow Americans and to facilitate communication with the folks back home. As far as foreign policy went, there was none to conduct—in Kuwait, there was no longer a host government and in Iraq there was no access. It was different in Washington where Iraq's ambassador, Mohamed al-Mashat, was repeatedly called on the carpet only to repeatedly accuse the United States of crimes and conspiracy. Not a single Iraqi citizen in the United States was harmed in any way—unlike the human shields and hostages in the Mideast.

War of nerves

One by one, other embassies in Kuwait ran out of food and water and had to be abandoned—the diplomats given safe haven to depart by gleeful Iraqis who wanted to close all the embassies in Kuwait.

By mid-October, Howell and company were down to a three- to four-week supply of canned tuna fish and rice, and were almost out of fuel for their generator. They had run out of bathing water and were forced to scrupulously ration what they had to drink. In one of those tender little victories, Howell and members of his staff went to work with shovels to dig a well behind the ambassador's residence. As a result, they had enough water to be able to wash cars, take showers and water the garden. But they were still running out of food.

"[Our] Kuwaiti embassy is being starved," President Bush said. "The people out there are not being resupplied. The American flag is flying over the Kuwait embassy and our people inside are being starved by a brutal dictator. And do you think I'm concerned about it? You're darned right I am. And what I'm going to do about it—let's just wait and see . . ."

One step Bush took was to seek a United Nations resolution demanding that Iraq allow resupply of embassies in Kuwait. It seemed certain Iraq would ignore the resolution. So another flashpoint was at hand—the volatile moment when the United States might seek to transport provisions to its Kuwait embassy and Iraq might step in to prevent it.

Bush, Baker, Cheney and others in Washington pondered a plan to sail a merchant ship into Kuwait city where, in theory at least, the vessel could dock within a few hundred feet of the embassy compound. Iraqi troops would, of course, be able to prevent the ship from un-

101

loading—but if they did, it could be the occasion for military action.

While a test of wills persisted, Americans drilled in the desert.

"Now that we're here, let's nuke 'im," someone had scribbled on the wall inside the crude wood-and-canvas latrine used by Specialist (SPC) Chris Fadness and other 82nd Airborne tankers. In a different hand, in felt-tip red, another soldier had written, "Now that we're here, let's go home." With the initial problem of getting there behind, the sentiments of Americans in uniform were diverse and compelling.

Whiling away days and nights on the Saudi desert, many shared the opinion, also popular back home, that it was time for decisive action against Saddam Hussein and that sooner was better than later. Others, especially officers and NCOs, understood fully that getting there was only part of the solution and that fighting skills needed to be honed. As late as mid-October, ten weeks into Desert Shield, troops needed training, equipment needed to be acclimated, and the specter of chemical warfare loomed over everything. In the 82nd latrine, a third outhouse poet had struck. "It won't be a walk in the park," began the graffiti, repeating Iraqi's warning against any American invasion, "but let's make Saddam Hussein glow in the dark."

"We're getting into the period of maximum danger," warned Professor Michael Hudson, expert on Arab and Middle East affairs with Georgetown University, speaking in mid-October. Hudson warned that only sudden and

With most of the moving-in accomplished, American troops set up positions and practice fighting in the desert. These 24th Infantry Division soldiers practice *planting an M–21 mine.* US Army/Gil High via Michael Green

overwhelming action would work. President Bush was leaving no room for compromise and Saddam Hussein showed no sign of backing down. The Iraqi population, Hudson warned, would fight bravely. Even if the Americans won a war which could cost up to 15,000 casualties, there would be a "political Chernobyl effect" in the Mideast. Radical opposition to an American presence would not end even with an end to Saddam Hussein. Like many experts including some distinguished military analysts, Hudson seemed to be warning that Americans shouldn't fight because it would be difficult.

Whether Americans on the Saudi desert were going to make Iraq's Hussein glow or not, they were going to need a little help from their friends. While attention focused on other is-sues—hostages trapped in Iraq, diplomats stranded in Kuwait, the Americans' problems with training, with equipment, with chemical warfare—few noticed that when the Bush administration pulled off a remarkable job of conjuring up military support from other nations. Shoulder to shoulder with Desert Shield's Americans were soldiers of numerous other nations.

Allied support

The British were ready. They always were. They'd fought for their lives in 1940 while some Americans waffled—arguing that the issue was not clearcut—and other Americans stayed asleep, not to awaken until Pearl Harbor. In 1982, while Americans waffled once again and apologists sought to inject shades of meaning

Guns and equipment are checked and rechecked to ensure that they are ready for instant action. US Army/Gil High via Michael Green

into the stark black-and-white of freedom versus tyranny, the British carried out a daring military campaign in the Falklands and defeated one of the clearest challenges to freedom in recent history.

Now, close on the heels of the first American components, British military people moved again. Over the weekend of August 11 and 12, 1990, Tornado F.3 fighter-interceptors of the Royal Air Force's No. 29 Squadron were rushed from Akrotiri, Cyprus, to a Saudi air base. They were soon joined by aircraft and personnel from other squadrons. The RAF Tornados, together with Saudi ADV Tornados (air defense variant), joined the early-arrival F-15C Eagles of the 1st Tactical Fighter Wing in flying 24-hour-a-day air defense patrols along Saudi Arabia's borders with Iraq and Kuwait while guarding the principal airfield where people and equipment arrived around the clock.

Thirteen RAF Jaguar GR.1As from No. 6 Squadron and five from No. 41 squadron, hastily repainted in a light desert camouflage scheme, quickly joined the Tornados in the Persian gulf region. Nimrod maritime patrol aircraft armed with Harpoon missiles began patrolling the Gulf itself. Hercules transports and Tornado GR.1 ground-attack warplanes followed. The mood among RAF personnel was strikingly like that of the Americans. Uprooted suddenly with virtually no notice, they exhibited pride, courage and readiness.

Operation Granby was the name for the British effort. Though they did not span distances as great as the Americans, the British had some solid experience under their belts with their very successful 1982 operation in the Falklands. They, too, mounted an impressive airlift. The British were not supermen, however, and it was not true, as reported in the London *Daily Mail* on October 13, that "six Hercules aircraft left Gutersloh yesterday carrying 3,500 Army vehicles, 1,000 containers, and nearly 30,000 tons of stores."

Great Britain also committed four major warships and three minesweepers. The latter were very important, for the US Navy had been caught with no minesweepers in the region.

France contributed the aircraft carrier *Clemenceau*, four other warships and Foreign Legion troops from Djibouti to a force which eventually reached 9,000. Between August and October 1990, the French presence grew to ten warships, twenty-four fighter planes, seventy-two helicopters and 200 armored vehicles.

Other warships came from Australia, Belgium, Greece, West Germany (which became a united Germany in October), Italy, the Netherlands and Turkey. Even the Soviet Union made an early promise to commit two warships to the Persian Gulf, then decided to use "other methods" to support the widespread call for Iraq to pull out of Kuwait.

Egyptian, Syrian and Moroccan troops had important symbolic value—evidence that fellow Arabs had the courage to confront Saddam Hussein. But they also had important military significance, making up during the early days of the buildup for American shortcomings in heavy assets and equipment, especially armor. Egyptian President Hosni Mubarak dispatched 2,000 ground soldiers at the very beginning, and bolstered their numbers as Desert Shield continued. Over time, Egypt's contribution reached 14,000 troops in Saudi Arabia plus 3,000 to 5,000 troops and antiaircraft missiles in other Persian Gulf states.

Even more surprising was the contribution by Syria's President Assad—a frequent critic of The United States' Middle East policy—who provided 4,000 troops initially and promised 12,000 more over time. Though there were some signs Assad might waiver, Syria's earnestness was proven in October with the first arrivals of main battle tanks—ironically, the same Soviet-made T-54 and T-72s which were among the most numerous of Iraq's tanks.

Turkey, a NATO member with a border on Iraq, earmarked 5,000 ground troops for possible duty in Saudi Arabia and dispatched two frigates to sail in the Gulf. Turkey also provided basing for American F-16s and F-111s.

In due course, the British contribution reached 16,000 troops and support staff including the 9,500-strong 7th Armored Brigade, the "Desert Rats," and 120 tanks (operating under command of the US Marines) plus forty combat aircraft and twelve ships.

Perhaps with the firing of the US Air Force's General Michael J. Dugan in mind, British officials gave a very cautious briefing on how hostilities might unfold. They refused to acknowledge that a recapture of Kuwait would require amphibious landings but revealed what was scarcely news—that any fighting would include attacks on air bases inside Iraq to establish the air superiority crucial to victory. Air Chief Marshall Sir Patrick Hine told reporters just what the Iraqis themselves had said—that war with Iraq would not be a walk in the park. "We have to make the point that a conflict will not be a cheap business in terms of casualties," said Sir Patrick. "It will be a very serious matter."

Command and control

From the beginning, the sudden buildup of military force on the desert created a problem which dampened the fighting spirit of warriors since the beginning of time. Simply put, the problem is, "Who's in charge?" History has shown that armies win battles only when they have a single, clearly visible leader—a Napoleon or a MacArthur.

Even if only American forces were considered, all problems could not be solved by reminding everybody that their boss was General H. Norman Schwarzkopf. At the principal airbase in eastern Saudi Arabia, Colonel John M. McBroom's F-15C Eagle wing was the "host unit," which meant in effect that it owned the base and that other components, including US Army avia-

24th Infantry Division soldiers discuss strategy in the Saudi desert. US Army via Michael Green

tion and Military Airlift Command people, were "tenants." Who, then, was to make routine decisions that affected everyone on the air base, such as how to manage security or how to dispose of the garbage? In theory, this might fall on Colonel McBroom, whose real job was to lead fighter pilots in battle. In fact, relationships were complex and diffuse—reporters being escorted by a MAC officer were accosted for stepping into the fighter wing's "tent city," while visitors to the fighter wing could find no MAC officer to talk to.

Who's in charge? In modern warfare, command and control relationships often form an intricate maze: Who reports to whom? In Pentagon briefings, officers sidestep the question by aiming their stem-like pointers (those batons, so essential to *any* briefing) at organization charts, called "wiring diagrams," which use squares and arrows to show how one organization, one leader, is related to another. Wiring diagrams are a deeply-rooted staple of military life—preparing them takes up millions of person-hours per year—and they are almost totally useless. If US Central Command's General Schwarzkopf was in command of all American troops, what about the British troops? The French? The Saudis?

The multinational force on the Saudi desert was, in fact, operating under an unorthodox

An 82nd Airborne paratrooper sets up a defensive flanking position with his M-249 machine gun. US Army/SSG Corkran via Michael Green

arrangement in which there was no supreme commander. There were two main chiefs, General Schwarzkopf and Saudi Lieutenant General Prince Khalid bin Sultan. Schwarzkopf, of course, headed up the 240,000 US troops, as well as the British "Desert Rats." Khalid, in turn, commanded Saudi, Syrian, Egyptian and Moroccan troops. And the French were led by General Michel Roquejeoffe, who took his orders from Paris.

The setup reflected the sensitive nature of hosting westerners on Arab soil to confront another Arab country—to say nothing of language barriers and cultural differences—but it also left unclear the question of who would lead troops in battle. Schwarzkopf and Khalid met daily and were in close touch with Roquejeoffe. Together, the generals made plans to run a war from a secret US-Saudi operations post in Schwarzkopf's headquarters in the desert. It was not a command arrangement that Napoleon would have liked. "We have to go with what we've got," one of Schwarzkopf's deputies explained. "There was no rehearsal for this. We've never done it before."

By the end of the first ten weeks, American troop strength reached 240,000. These troops were supported by more than 800 main battle tanks, 800 combat aircraft based in Saudi Arabia and on four Navy carriers—including USS *Midway* (CV-41), home-ported in Japan, which came on station in October—and hundreds of antitank and transport helicopters.

In place on the ground was the equivalent of six divisions, the largest American deployment since Vietnam. It was anchored by the 82nd and 101st Airborne, 24th Infantry Division (Mechanized), and a composite division of the 197th Mechanized Infantry Brigade, 1st Cavalry Brigade, and 3rd Armored Regiment. There were also 45,000 Marines, including 11,000 in the expeditionary brigade on assault ships in the Gulf.

Together with Allied troops, this was the force which had been envisioned by Pentagon planners when they launched Desert Shield in the wake of Iraq's August 2, 1990, invasion of Kuwait. It was time, in mid-October, to announce to the world that Desert Shield was finished and that the air- and sealift had gotten the needed force in place, as intended.

Larger force

But suddenly, the planned number of troops was not enough. The Iraqi army was a beehive of activity as new forces were moved into, or close to, occupied Kuwait. The size of the Iraqi threat had now more than doubled, and American officers questioned whether their own troop strength had reached the level required to offset the 430,000 troops Saddam Hussein had scattered in and around Kuwait.

Ten weeks into Desert Shield, having reached the target of 240,000, the Pentagon abruptly made known new plans—based on second thoughts—to increase the force by 200,000 *more* troops. In addition, the armored force which relied mainly on the M1 Abrams would be bolstered with huge numbers of the more advanced M1A1.

Desert Shield had pretty well cleaned out all of the forces which Americans had available for contingencies. If 200,000 *more* troops were going to be needed, where would they come from? Now, the impact of having the smallest army in decades was felt. There simply was no place to get any more troops without doing the unprecedented.

For the first time since the earliest dawnings of the Cold War, the Pentagon would pull troops out of Europe.

Of greatest importance, Defense Secretary Cheney, General Schwarzkopf and others settled on a major switch in tank deployments. Hundreds of M1A1 Abrams main battle tanks, with their bigger 120 mm guns and new chemical protection systems, would be moved from Europe to supplant or replace the older M1 Abrams tanks with 105 mm guns. At the start of Desert Shield, military leaders decided that the fastest way to deliver heavy armor was to dispatch US based units, all with older tanks. In Europe, untouched by Mideast developments, were no fewer than 1,790 of the newer M1A1s, each weighing 63 tons, with a crew of four, and with a 2,200-yard reach for its gunner.

The Army wanted M1A1s in Saudi Arabia for three key reasons. The M1A1 had a more sophisticated, more accurate fire-control system than earlier M1 or M60 tanks. The newer tank with its more powerful gun was also a better match for Iraq's best tanks, the Soviet-made T-72s with 125 mm guns. Finally, the M1A1 also would fight better if chemical weapons were unleashed, thanks to its "over-pressure" air-conditioning system enabling soldiers to stay cool and protected from poison gas.

The concern over training felt by many officers was one for which no simple solutions lay at hand. The 24th Infantry's Michelle Curphey noticed one sergeant repeatedly ordering his troops to, "get *serious*, people!" The order was repeated so often, without any specific instruction behind it, that it lost credibility. Other NCOs and officers trained by example, leading their troops through maneuvers with the emphasis on rapid movement, surprise and survivability. Much of the American planning and training took place at night—which was when the Americans wanted to fight and would fight best.

Equipment problems

Among the many items of equipment accused of vulnerability in the harsh desert conditions, night-vision goggles (NVGs) were the most

A paratrooper signals forward another squad member from his position in the Saudi desert. US Army/ SSG Corkran via Michael Green

controversial. Some critics picked on NVGs as a shining example of the American infatuation with high tech—looking to technology to win wars when simpler solutions were more effective. Others argued that NVGs were a good idea, but those issued to US troops didn't work well enough.

Several types of NVGs, making use of infrared sensors to transform night into day, were in use with helicopter crews, tank drivers and some highly specialized infantry troops. The ability to use NVGs and to fly scout and tank-killing helicopters under cover of darkness gave US forces a big edge over Iraq's huge army and tank arsenal. But sand dunes lacked the texture of topographical features elsewhere, and even when NVGs were working properly a helicopter pilot could fly into a mound of sand simply because it produced no shadow.

The NVGs almost always *did* work properly, and mishaps were usually caused by faulty tactics. Early in Desert Shield it became obvious—there were five night-time crashes to prove it, none with fatalities—that the OH-58 Kiowa scout helicopter had to be manned by two pilots, not one, giving the crew more eyes to peer through dusty sand and spot dunes. The army changed its tactics so that new pilots were restricted to certain training areas until they became used to the harsh terrain, whereupon

A picture the American public may not be fully ready for: members of the armed forces suited up to cope with the threat of chemical warfare. Taken in the desert of the Persian Gulf region during Desert Shield, this view of Americans in chemical gear is typical. Department of Defense

they graduated and flew over more complicated terrain. Newly arrived pilots were prohibited from flying below 150 feet (46.44 meters) to reduce the risk of striking a dune.

Helicopters, aircraft and vehicles showed themselves highly vulnerable to heat and sand. The army had designed an effective filter to keep grit out of the intakes and exhausts of its helicopter engines but did not have enough of them. Helicopter rotors proved vulnerable to damage from sand blown through the air by the ever-present winds. At one juncture, an army aviation officer claimed that his AH-64 Apache helicopters were up to operational readiness seventy-five percent of the time—and was immediately descended upon by critics, who thought twenty-five percent down was too much.

On aircraft and on the ground, the acid in batteries fizzled and fried in the Saudi heat, causing them to explode. On the F-15C Eagle, gritty particles of sand ate into seals on the

US Army soldiers in Saudi Arabia can never relax their guard completely. They carry weapons and chemical warfare masks even while exercising. As Desert Shield dragged on without the sudden, sharp conflict that had seemed possible in the beginning, officers and NCOs struggled to keep up the morale of soldiers in the field, with a little help from a flood of supporting mail sent by Americans everywhere. US Army

aircraft fuselage, requiring costly and frequent maintenance. One model of field radio could not be used in the desert because its metal handle became too hot to grasp. Michelle Curphey's fellow soldiers in the 24th Mechanized Infantry wrapped other radios in burlap to keep them from overheating. Still, without protection in the worst of hot temperatures, batteries exploded, the metal frames of some vehicles buckled and rifle magazines warped. The passage of time solved some of these problems—by October, it was not as hot—and hard-working soldiers and marines found solutions for others.

Not all of the problems were caused by desert conditions. The army fired civil engineer Calvin J. Weber for pointing out that about two-thirds of the 300 UH–60A/L Black Hawk helicopters in Saudi Arabia lacked special engine attachments intended to hide their exhaust from heat-seeking missiles. The army simply didn't have enough of these mufflerlike devices. They were designed to cool the exhaust before it leaves the powerplants and to hide the red-hot turbine blades from the missiles. Critics argued that AH–64 Apaches were also too vulnerable to shoulder-mounted missiles, like the Soviet-built SA–14 believed to be in Iraq's arsenal.

There are numerous stories of individual Americans struggling to cope with these equipment problems—and triumphing over them. At Aberdeen Proving Ground in Maryland, a team of artillery experts found a new way of crating and packing artillery shells, preventing ammunition boxes from buckling and warping in the Saudi heat. At Fort Irwin, California, a handful of aviators wrote a new training manual for helicopter flying in hot weather—virtually overnight. In the Saudi desert itself, mechanics and maintenance people were the real heroes of the Army and Marine Corps, getting full performance out of their Hummers, Abrams and Sheridans even when logic called for the vehicles to break down and die.

Nuclear, biological and chemical warfare

Some items of equipment worked better than others, and there could be no doubt that some weapons were simply too heat sensitive for

An inevitable Americanism: in tent city amid an unusual fog, a crude signboard points the way to everybody's hometown. Robert F. Dorr

111

the desert. Hanging over everything else, though, was the new ingredient in this crisis which made it so different from all others in the past—the threat of nuclear, biological and chemical warfare (NBC).

Since early in the Cold War, American service people rehearsed the craft of war while wearing NBC warfare suits or, at least, gas masks. Chemical weapons were, and still are, integral to the arsenal the Soviets would unleash in any conflict with NATO armies. War in Europe would require Allied air bases to absorb Soviet strikes with bombs and rockets having chemical warheads.

In their new and different setting in the Persian Gulf region, hard-pressed officers and NCOs—looking at flat stretches of empty sand and struggling to create real, credible defenses—were forced to devote precious time and effort to getting troops ready to don NBC gear on sudden notice. Even if Iraq never let loose any killing agent from its chemical chamber of horrors, the threat by itself soaked up enormous American resources, time and effort.

The chemical threat was viewed differently among the units, however. At a Saudi airfield (where warplanes luxuriated out of doors, wingtip to wingtip, as if no one had ever heard of strafing), Air Force security police crammed khaki burlap sacks containing NBC gear into a corner of their office—up to several miles from men and women who guarded the gates. Aboard the carrier *Kennedy*, deck crews drilled in gas masks which (unlike full NBC gear) offered only partial defense against chemical attack—but those below decks stowed the masks in their lockers, far from their work stations. On the desert itself, where soldiers and marines might face a night armored assault in heat and fog, NBC protective gear received a much more urgent priority.

Chris Fadness, Michelle Curphey and other US Army soldiers were told repeatedly that they

A US air base on October 12, 1990, had few bunkers to protect military people in case of air attack. This sandbagged bunker a few feet from the flight line was nicknamed Heartbreak Hotel. Robert F. Dorr

were supposed to have their chemical warfare gear readily at hand and to be prepared to have themselves fully enclosed inside NBC protective garment in eight minutes. In spite of decades of Cold War preparations, many had never seen NBC garb before they reached the Mideast.

Nor had most of them ever learned much about what they were protecting themselves against.

Iraq's arsenal included a little of everything.

Nuclear

The Pentagon believed that Saddam Hussein didn't have atomic bombs yet, though he was working on it. On June 7, 1981, Israeli F-16s loaded with fuel and bombs, escorted by F-15 Eagles, flew 1,000 miles (1,610 kilometers) to pulverize Iraq's Osirak (Tamuz) nuclear reactor near Baghdad, dealing nuclear program a stunning setback. At the time, the Israeli raid had seemed brash—the very kind of nose-thumbing toward civil behavior of which Iraq now stood accused—but now it seemed a favor. Though many kinds of protective gear could shield an American soldier from after-effects such as fallout, there is no protection against the blast or radiation of an atomic explosion.

Biological

Almost overlooked amid heightened concern about chemical warfare, Iraq turned the practice of medicine akilter and developed artillery shells and bombs to spread disease.

Some of Iraq's research focused on anthrax, an infectious disease of cattle and sheep that is fatal to humans.

But Iraq was also developing weapons using botulism—based on the most toxic poison known to man (a bacteria in the genus clostridium, related to the cause of tetanus). Both anthrax and botulin can be spread through the air with an airburst by an artillery shell or bomb. As one expert points out, "Even a few grams [of botulin] in the water supply will wipe out a town the size of Gettysburg, Pennsylvania." Time and

Even though the hottest part of the year has passed, the troops still require millions of gallons of water per day. Part of it is provided by the Army's reverse osmosis water purifying units. US Army/Gil High via Michael Green

dilution will nullify the effect of both anthrax and botulin bacteria. So, too, will the ever-shifting winds of the gritty Saudi desert. But a simple gas mask affords no protection at all, and some estimates hold that a full NBC suit can be effective only if worn for twelve hours on a battlefield where bacteria has been unleashed.

Chemical

More likely to be employed against Americans than either nuclear or biological weaponry, Iraq's chemical threat is divided into nerve and mustard agents.

Even at the height of the Cold War, the superpowers resisted stockpiling nerve agents (the word "gas," usually used, is a misnomer) such as sarin, which the Iraqis possess. Invisible, tasteless and odorless, sarin and other nerve agents break down the chemical acetylcholine, which normally serves as a bridge between nerve synapses, throwing the nervous system out of whack and causing muscle spasms which lead to convulsions, respiratory failure, heart failure and death. "Think of the nervous system as a trolley line," says an expert. "When the brain tells a nerve to do something—to move a muscle, let's say—it sends a signal in the form of an impulse. That impulse is like a passenger on a trolley. It needs to make a transfer to another rail line to reach its destination. The nerve synapse is that transfer point. Acetylcholine is a conducting medium enabling the impulse to jump from one nerve ending to another. The nerve *agent*—one of them is called acetylchole esterase—will break down acetylcholine and make it impossible for the nerve impulse to complete its transfer. This causes the whole system to break down and you die. Even if a tiny droplet gets on your skin, you die. If there's a tear in your sleeve or a hole in your shoe, you die."

Troops rely on chemical alarms for warning of nerve agents and carry syrettes containing an antidote, atrophine. Soldiers using atrophine give themselves the initial injection but require medical help, tying up resources.

Though a simple gas mask is not usually enough to protect against nerve agents, full NBC attire is. Fortunately, the horror of nerve gas is less than fully practical on a vast, open battle-field where the winds quickly disperse the agents.

Far more dangerous to American troops—and used in the past by Iraq—was that old horror from World War I, often called mustard gas but better described as a blister agent.

Blister agents are a thick liquid, either colorless or dark brown, that can blister the skin or damage the eyes. This vesicant, or irritant, if inhaled can blister the lungs, throat and trachea. Exposure is fatal to less than five percent of those caught unprotected on the battlefield, but an army can be incapacitated by malaise, vomiting and fever. Even a simple gas mask is some help against blister agents and full NBC attire provides complete protection.

NBC garb

Though various gas masks were in use, soldiers and marines in Saudi Arabia were equipped with—and kept at hand—full NBC garb which enclosed them totally against the outside world. One version of this chemical warfare gear used the M-17 black butyl rubber mask, or the updated Air Force silicon version known as MCU-2P, together with protective garment, boots and gloves. The suit is heavy, bulky and hot. Once inside, soldiers cannot tell each other apart—degrading the effectiveness of leaders. Furthermore, the typical NBC suit can only be used once and is not designed for laundering or re-issue.

In the middle of Operation Desert Shield, American troops generally were able to use their NBC gear and to practice fighting in it, including practicing house-to-house combat. Leaders worried that inattention, error or sloth—not the equipment itself—could result in casualties during any chemical attack. Those who operated in tanks and armored vehicles at least had air conditioning to aid their comfort while wearing the heavy garb, and some could look forward to the expected arrival of M1A1 Abrams tanks, which could fight in a chemical environment without its crew wearing protection.

Navy and Air Force flight crew members adjusted well to their very different set of NBC gear consisting of MBU-13P gas mask and rubber hood, their standard, fire-retardant flight suit and a charcoal-coated, cotton under-garment. Ten weeks into Desert Shield, the Air Force began to equip flight crews with 5,300 new protective integrated hood/mask units (PIHM), designed by Boeing, which included a blower to ventilate the mask and maintained a positive pressure inside.

Why so much attention to grotesque weapons no one had used in World War II, Korea or Vietnam, and which American officers had not even considered in Lebanon, Grenada or Panama? After all, most nations had quietly honored an informal ban against unleashing nuclear, chemical and biological horrors in war. Even Hitler and his World War II generals had held back their stock of blister agents. There were exceptions—Italy's use of blister agents during its 1938 invasion of Ethiopa and the Soviet's use of a biological agent, "yellow rain," in Afghanistan—but even in desperate situations, most decision makers had refrained.

Iraq was different. Pentagon officers believed that Iraq would not hesitate to use biological and chemical weapons. In any new conflict, Iraq would be fighting for survival. "If war does come," warned Pentagon officer Lieutenant Colonel Nathan Shumway, "it will be World War III as far as Saddam Hussein is concerned. He will hold nothing back. He must defeat an enormous force which includes hundreds of thousands of Americans—or he dies." Saddam Hussein's warriors had already used blister agents in the eight-year war with Iran and (in an especially cruel action) against Iraq's own Kurdish population.

How effective, then, would these hideous weapons be? American forces hoped they would not have to find out, but the experts viewed these weapons more as a nuisance than a threat. On the desert, biological and blister agents would dissipate rapidly. General Schwarzkopf's troops were geared up for highly mobile desert warfare, not for sitting still as defenseless Iraqi Kurds had done. Most Pentagon planners believed that Hussein's chemical arsenal will carry out a role similar to that of the biplanes used by the North Koreans in the 1950 to 1953 Korean conflict as nocturnal pests which made plenty of

As this book went to press, no one was sure whether the soldiers of Desert Shield would be forced to fight a war. But they are *ready.* US Army/CPT Mike Edrington via Michael Green

noise and dropped a few bombs: Their military utility was marginal, but they were a tremendous nuisance, making it necessary to divert great resources to defending against them. The nuisance factor could not be discounted. After all, if Iraq achieved nothing more than to force the United States to provide 240,000 people with NBC suits, it had created a monumental distraction.

Would the United States retaliate in kind? Operation Desert Shield occurred just as the United States was disposing of its small, aging stock of chemical weapons—transporting them from storage in Germany to disposal at John-ston Island in the Pacific. These artillery shell warheads had been in storage for many years and were considered too old to be safe to use, and the United States had not manufactured new chemical warheads for decades. The United States had already disposed of its biological agents. Fort Deatrick, Maryland, where anthrax, botulin and other toxins were tossed around in test tubes in the 1950s had long since been converted to other, peaceful forms of medical research. In the last years of the Cold War, American and NATO doctrine held that any Soviet attack would involve massive use of chemical weapons, but that the Allied response

Whatever else Desert Shield accomplished, it proved that on zero notice the United States could mount the greatest airlift of people, supplies and equipment in world history—spanning enormous distances, arriving in unfamiliar locations and disgorging a force that in due course numbered more than 240,000 people. Whatever was to come next, Desert Shield ranked as a towering achievement of the American armed forces—and the airlifter, like this C–141B Starlifter, deserved much of the credit. US Air Force

would not employ chemicals. The Allies might, however, be forced into early employment of tactical *nuclear* weapons against a Soviet onslaught.

Big bomb

Would the United States use nuclear weapons against Iraq? A survey showed that while most Americans were extremely skittish about their own soldiers bleeding and dying, fewer than twenty percent felt any qualms about using nuclear weapons against Iraq. A British officer said in public that if his forces were attacked with chemical weapons they would not hesitate to use tactical nuclear warheads. Further comment was quickly hushed, and American officers said nothing. United States policy had long been known in jargon as NCND—we would "neither confirm nor deny" the presence of nuclear weapons at any specific location. It was unlikely that Saudi Arabia or other Gulf states would permit American atomic bombs on their soil, but it seemed fairly certain that the four aircraft carriers in the region carried what the Pentagon euphemistically called "special weapons."

On balance the NBC threat was not enough to alter the fundamentals at stake in Desert Shield. The men and women of the US armed forces, many of them hearing about the threat for the first time, deserved high marks for training with their equipment, getting to know it well, and remaining ready to use it. In actual combat, Murphy's law applied—anything that could go wrong, would go wrong—and some casualties were certain to result from a degraded ability to fight while wearing the NBC suit. But this was part of the equation.

As with everything else they did on little notice and under enormous pressure during Desert Shield, members of the armed forces adapted quickly, improvised and pulled off a super job confronting the NBC threat. It was like every job they took on, from Green Ramp to the Saudi desert. Members of the armed forces gave us better than we deserved. The lowest ranking among them deserved more from us—not just cookies from home, but a serious pay check. They were willing to face death on the desert at a time when we, back home, were not even strong enough to straighten out our government's fiscal mess.

In Desert Shield, many items of hardware and weaponry had stood up well to their first real test—and some hadn't. But it was clear that we were squandering too many dollars on high-ticket, high-tech weapons and not enough on simple, practical items of equipment. One Navy officer said he would have "killed" to get the improved A-6F Intruder fighter-bomber which would have been in service in 1990, had it not been canceled in 1988 to make way for the stealth A-12—which was many years away from flying, let alone entering service. "It doesn't matter how good a thing is if you have to fight a war today and it isn't coming until tomorrow," asserted the Navy officer.

Whatever might happen with the military hardware items, the important thing was that *people* in American uniform had proven themselves. As a sailor on the *Wisconsin* put it, "Saddam Hussein is going to back down or get his rear end kicked." At the end of the period covered by this report, it seemed certain that the sailor was right—and there appeared the first, tentative signs that people in Baghdad were squirming.

Afterword

Was it one of those silly-season news stories that flicker and fade, or did it *mean* something? In mid-October 1990, a news report claimed that Iraq's Saddam Hussein recounted a dream in which the prophet Mohammed told him: "I see your missiles pointed wrongly," meaning in the wrong direction.

Like their Saudi hosts and Iraqi adversaries, Americans in uniform have an abiding respect for religion. Few people of any of these nationalities could have felt much enthusiasm for using the prophet to float a trial balloon. But American barracks humor can be irreverent, and the American men and women of Desert Shield were entitled to claim that if Mohammed was decreeing a change in course, their stand in the desert had given Mohammed a little nudge. It remained to be seen whether the news story marked a turn of the tide.

Other issues, too, remained to be resolved. The performance of American men and women in deploying to the Saudi desert was not one of them, for the evidence was in, and Desert Shield was a triumph. Left to be resolved was the question of how the new breed of warriors in today's American armed forces would acquit themselves in modern warfare—but if their performance during Desert Shield offered any clue, the American public had gotten the professional force it wanted. It was time for the American populace to serve these professionals as well as they served the American populace—not with praise, or letters from home, or even water pis-

tols, but with a paycheck that measured up and with the promise of a secure career, budget cuts or no budget cuts.

Desert Shield had worked. President George Bush's national security advisor said, accurately, that the US deployment to the Persian Gulf was one of the smoothest military operations in memory and that it was no accident: it happened because of planning, training and—budget cuts or not—the expenditure of defense dollars.

When this story went to press, no one—except, perhaps, a deity—could say whether we would have peace or war. But for ten weeks, while a "window of opportunity" beckoned Saddam Hussein, no attack had been made on Saudi Arabia. More important, other glimmerings indicated that Iraq was seriously considering backing out—searching for a face-saving way to pull out of Kuwait. If so, it would be the first time in many years that Americans employed force of arms to successfully achieve their goals.

Standing in the heat at the principal Saudi air base, ALCE Captain Christopher Mardis watched a C–5B Galaxy taxi by and spoke of his pride in his nation, in his buddies and in the airlift that made it happen. "We have achieved something unique," Mardis said. "These men and women made it happen. A lesser group of men and women could not have done it."

At the same Saudi airfield, I saw the heroes of the Desert Shield airlift at their best and, too, at their worst—some exhausted, irritable, keyed up, others cool and competent. I saw sweat, sacrifice, hard work, horseplay, some classic American bitching and an achievement that will rank with anything our armed forces have done in our history.

It was not too early to say that they had proven themselves—our new breed of volunteers, including marrieds, minorities and women—on the battlefield. It was not too early to say that most of our items of equipment performed as the brochure said; the F-15C Eagle fighter, the Aegis-class guided missile warship, the M1 Abrams battle tank would perform on the battlefield. In ten weeks, we had succeeded beyond anything we might have hoped for back at the start, on that distant August night at Green Ramp.

Chronology

August 2
Iraq invades Kuwait.

August 7
United States embarks on Operation Desert Shield with the stated purpose of defending Saudi Arabia and forcing Iraq to withdraw from Kuwait.

Forty-eight F-15C/D Eagle air superiority fighters of the 1st Tactical Fighter Wing's 27th and 71st squadrons under Colonel John M. "Boomer" McBroom begin deploying to Saudi Arabia on only hours' notice.

USS *Independence* (CV-62) carrier battle group arrives on station in the Gulf of Oman.

USS *Dwight D. Eisenhower* (CVN-69) carrier battle group transits the Suez Canal en route to the Red Sea.

USS *Saratoga* (CV-60) carrier battle group and battleship USS *Wisconsin* (BB-64) depart East Coast en route to Desert Shield region.

August 10
F-16C/D Fighting Falcon jet fighters from the 363rd Tactical Reconnaissance Wing, Shaw AFB, South Carolina, and C-130E Hercules cargo aircraft from the 317th Tactical Airlift Wing, Pope AFB, North Carolina, begin arriving in the Desert Shield region.

US Navy hospital ships *Mercy* (T-AH-19) and *Comfort* (T-AH-20) are activated for deployment to the Middle East.

Troops and vehicles of the 24th Infantry Division (Mechanized) move by road from Fort Stewart, Georgia, to Savannah, Georgia, to begin loading aboard the fast US sealift ship *Capella* (T-AKR-293).

Pentagon deploys a pool of reporters to cover Desert Shield, arranging visits for some reporters aboard the Aegis cruiser USS *Antietam* (CG-54) in the Persian Gulf and the aircraft carrier USS *Independence* (CV-62) in the Gulf of Oman.

August 11
The 1st Marine Division, Camp Pendleton, California, and 101st Airborne Division (Air Assault), Fort Campbell, Kentucky, begin moving to embarkation points for deployment to the Middle East.

The 82nd Airborne Division paratroopers, F-16s from Shaw and C-130s from Pope continue to arrive.

August 12
F-15E Strike Eagles of the 4th Tactical Fighter Wing's 336th Squadron from Seymour Johnson AFB, North Carolina, begin deployment.

Army's 11th Air Defense Artillery Brigade, Fort Bliss, Texas, equipped with Patriot and Stinger missiles, arrives in the Middle East.

August 13
USNS *Comfort* sails from Norfolk, Virginia.

USNS *Capella* sails from Savannah with vehicles and equipment of the 24th Infantry Division (Mechanized). USNS *Bellatrix* (T-AKR-288) and USNS *Altair* (T-AKR-291) continue loading additional 24th people and gear.

KC-10 and KC-135 tankers, RC-135 reconnaissance aircraft and E-3A Sentry airborne warning and control system (AWACS) aircraft arrive in the Middle East in support of Desert Shield.

USS *Wisconsin* transits Strait of Gibraltar en route to Persian Gulf.

Advance elements of the 1st Marine Expeditionary Force and 7th Marine Expeditionary Brigade arrive in Saudi Arabia. The 4th Marine Expeditionary Brigade, including parts of the 2nd Marine Division and Marine aircraft from Cherry Point, North Carolina, and New River, North Carolina, embark on thirteen amphibious ships.

August 15

USS *John F. Kennedy* (CV-67) and her carrier battle group sail from Norfolk. Included are the cruisers USS *Thomas P. Gates* (CG-51), USS *Mississippi* (CGN-41) and USS *San Jacinto* (CG-56). Scheduled to replace USS *Dwight D. Eisenhower*, the *Kennedy* battle group is sent forth before a decision has been made as to whether to bring *Ike* home.

USS *Saratoga* carrier battle group transits Strait of Gibraltar en route to eastern Mediterranean.

F-4G Phantom Wild Weasel jets designed to suppress enemy missile sites begin to deploy from George AFB, California, with the 35th Tactical Fighter Wing. F-117A stealth fighters from the 37th Wing at Tonopah, Nevada, also begin moving out, at least twenty-two of them en route to a stopover on the East Coast.

Elements of the 1st Marine Expeditionary Brigade located at Kaneohe Bay, Hawaii, begin moving out, some aboard C-5 transports that circumnavigated the globe to pick them up.

Additional Army units from Fort Bragg, North Carolina, and Fort Benning, Georgia, begin moving to the Middle East.

August 16

Pentagon announces thirteen ships from Norfolk deploying with the Norfolk-based 4th Marine Expeditionary Brigade. Included are the amphibious assault ships USS *Guam* (LPH-9), USS *Nassau* (LHA-4) and USS *Iwo Jima* (LPH-2), as well as transport and landing ships.

Army's 3rd Armored Cavalry Regiment, Fort Bliss, begins deployment to the Middle East.

President George Bush authorizes US forces to intercept ships carrying products and commodities bound to and from Kuwait and Iraq.

August 17

Army's 1st Cavalry Division and 2nd Armored Division, both at Fort Hood, Texas, begin deploying to Middle East.

Navy activates nine Ready Reserve Forces (RRFs) of ninety-six sealift vessels, which are maintained in a five-, ten- or twenty-day readiness status.

Air Force deploys four air transportable hospitals to the Middle East.

Two US ships intercept two Iraqi coastal ships. USS *England* (CG-22) and USS *Robert G. Bradley* (FFG-49) challenge the Iraqi ships, determine that they are empty and allow them to proceed.

Air Force activates stage 1 (the lowest stage) of the Civil Reserve Air Fleet (CRAF), requiring sixteen airlines to make up to thirty-eight aircraft available within 24 hours. It is the first CRAF call-up in history.

Battleship USS *Wisconsin* transits the Suez Canal en route to the Persian Gulf.

August 18

USS *Reid* (FFG-30) intercepts Iraqi tanker *Khanaquin* in the Gulf of Oman. After tanker refuses to halt, *Reid* fires six shots across its bow. USS *Robert G. Bradley* intercepts a second tanker and fires warning shots. Both tankers remain under way, under American surveillance.

USS *John F. Kennedy* carrier battle group reaches eastern Mediterranean.

Air Force KC-135 tankers from Mildenhall, England, and A-10 Warthog ground attack aircraft from Myrtle Beach, South Carolina, begin arriving at Middle East locations.

Army's 101st Aviation Brigade also begins arriving at Middle East sites.

August 19

Vice Admiral Henry H. Mauz, Jr., becomes commander, US Naval Forces Central Command, controlling all naval forces assigned to Central Command under General H. Norman Schwarzkopf in Persian Gulf region.

August 22

President George Bush orders certain military reserve members to active duty for the first time since the Vietnam War.

Navy begins deployment of four mine sweepers to the Persian Gulf area, which has been without mine-sweeping capability since the "reflagging" operations in the area two years earlier.

USS *Saratoga* carrier battle group transits Suez Canal en route to the Red Sea.

August 23

Air National Guard and Air Force Reserve units called to active duty include three C-141B Starlifter and two C-5A Galaxy squadrons, as well as airlift terminal and cargo managers.

Dozens of Naval Reserve units are called to active duty to provide port and harbor security, sealift support and medical services. Army artillery units from Fort Sill, Oklahoma, and medical units from West Germany begin deploying to the Middle East.

Air Force C-130E Hercules equipped with Adverse Weather Aerial Delivery System (AWADS), belonging to the 435th Tactical Airlift Wing at Rhein-Main, West Germany, begin deploying to the Desert Shield area.

West Germany provides ten *Fuchs* (Fox) chemical monitoring vehicles for use by the United States in Operation Desert Shield. Twenty more are provided on September 6.

August 24

USS *Wisconsin* transits Strait of Hormuz into Persian Gulf.

August 25

Air Force's 48th Tactical Fighter Wing at Lakenheath, England, begins deploying F-111F Aardvark fighter bombers, each carrying four 2,000 pound (907 kilogram) GBU-15 TV guided bombs, to a location in Saudi Arabia. Twenty aircraft are deployed, followed by eighteen more on September 2.

Dozens of Army National Guard and Army Reserve units are alerted for call-up to active duty.

August 26

General H. Norman Schwarzkopf moves his headquarters of US Central Command, responsible for operations in the Persian Gulf region, from Florida to Saudi Arabia.

Army corps support units at Fort Hood begin to deploy to the Middle East.

August 27

USNS *Altair* and USNS *Capella* arrive in Saudi Arabia carrying components of the 24th Infantry Division (Mechanized).

August 28

Iraq continues its build-up of forces facing Saudi Arabia, with about 150,000 troops in occupied Kuwait and another 115,000 posing a direct threat to Saudi Arabia, an increase of about 70,000 troops overall within a week.

August 30

USS *John F. Kennedy* carrier battle group transits Strait of Gibraltar en route to Persian Gulf.

Air Force F-16C Fighting Falcons from the 401st Tactical Fighter Wing deploy from Torrejon, Spain, to Qatar in support of Operation Desert Shield. This is one of the few occasions when the Pentagon identifies a country in the region that is not Saudi Arabia.

Army aviation and armor elements from West Germany begin movement to the Desert Shield region.

Three more Air Force Reserve airlift squadrons are called up to active duty.

Navy's Fleet Hospital Five, a 500 bed, land-based, mobile treatment facility, deploys medical and staff people to the Middle East.

August 31

USS *Biddle* (CG-34) intercepts and boards the Iraqi merchant vessel *Al Karamah*. Tanker is empty and is allowed to continue to Aqaba, Jordan.

September 1

USS *Dwight D. Eisenhower* and USS *Ticonderoga* (CG-47), finished with their cruise, transit Strait of Gibraltar returning to their US home ports.

September 4

Three Army Reserve intelligence units with Arab-speaking linguists are called to active duty along with two more Air Force Reserve airlift units.

In the Gulf of Oman, crewmen from the guided missile destroyer USS *Goldsborough* (DDG-20) board the Iraqi-registered merchant ship *Zanoobia* carrying a shipment of tea to Basra, Iraq, and divert the ship to a nonprohibited port.

Amphibious ships USS *Shreveport* (LPD-12), USS *Trenton* (LPD-14) and others carrying the 4th Marine Expeditionary Brigade transit the Suez Canal en route to Saudi Arabia.

Fast sealift cargo ship USS *Algol* (T-AKR-287) arrives in Saudi Arabia with elements of the 24th Infantry Division (Mechanized).

September 5

Naval Reserve calls to active duty 790 reservists from eighty-four units. Another 660 reservists from twenty-two more units are called a day later.

September 6

Amphibious ships USS *Nassau*, USS *Raleigh* (LPD-1) and others transit the Suez Canal carrying components of the 4th Marine Expeditionary Brigade.

Fast sealift cargo ship USNS *Denebola* (T-AKR-289) arrives in Saudi Arabia with elements of the 24th Infantry Division (Mechanized).

September 7

Amphibious ship USS *Okinawa* (LPH-3) and others arrive in Gulf of Oman carrying 13th Marine Expeditionary Unit.

USNS *Comfort* arrives in Gulf of Oman.

September 8

Amphibious ships USS *Iwo Jima*, USS *Guam* and others transit Suez Canal carrying elements of 4th Marine Expeditionary Brigade.

USS *Comfort* arrives in the Persian Gulf.

September 11

Amphibious ships with 4th Marine Expeditionary Brigade reach the Gulf of Oman.

Additional Army National Guard and Army Reserve call-ups bring the total in Operation Desert Shield to 7,456 people in ninety-four units.

Saudi Arabia grants permission to US forces to conduct live-fire exercises.

September 12

US Army recalls 500 retired personnel. This is the first time in history retired people have been called to active duty.

Naval Reserve calls to active duty 106 more reservists from sixteen units.

USS *Dwight D. Eisenhower* and USS *Ticonderoga* return to East Coast ports.

September 14

Four more Air Force Reserve squadrons, all operating C-141B Starlifters, are called to active duty.

Frigates USS *Brewton* (FF-1086) and HMAS *Darwin*, of the Royal Australian Navy, intercept Iraqi tanker *Al-Fao* in the Gulf of Oman. After several requests to permit boarding, *Brewton* fires the first warning shots from one of its .50 caliber (12.7 millimeter) machine guns. *Darwin* fires a second set of warning shots. A joint boarding party goes aboard *Al-Fao* and determines that it contains no prohibited cargo.

September 18

Pentagon says Iraq troop strength threatening Saudi Arabia is up to 360,000. Some tanks moved back. CBS says American plan to put forces in gulf area are two weeks behind schedule but will be completed in mid-October.

An 82nd Airborne soldier is wounded by friendly fire. A howitzer shell wounds another man. First losses to friendly fire occur.

September 19

Secretary of Defense Dick Cheney approves imminent danger pay of $110 per month for officers and enlisted people in the Persian Gulf region.

Twenty-eight additional Army National Guard members and 34 Army Reserve members are called to active duty.

September 21

Air Force calls up 890 additional reservists in six airlift units.

September 26

Six Marine Corps OV-10D Bronco observation aircraft from squadron VMO-2 at Camp Pendleton—one a last-minute substitute from VMO-1 at New River—arrive at a Persian Gulf airfield.

September 27

USS *Montgomery* (FF-1082) fires warning shots, then boards an Iraqi tanker in the Red Sea in what the Pentagon describes as the fourth such at-sea encounter. Finding the tanker empty, *Montgomery* permits it to pass.

September 30

Air Force F-15E Eagle 87-02030 crashes in the Middle East, killing two men on board.

October 8

RF-4C Phantom 64-1044 reconnaissance aircraft of the Alabama Air National Guard crashes in the Middle East, killing two men on board.

Two Marine Corps UH-1N Huey helicopters, 160178 and 160622, crash in the North Arabian Sea during a night flight from the USS *Okinawa*, killing eight people on board.

October 10

Air Force F-111F 74-0183 fighter-bomber of the 48th Fighter Bomber Wing crashes in the Middle East, killing two men on board.

October 15

Defense Secretary Dick Cheney announces that the number of Americans in the Persian Gulf region now exceeds 200,000. Experts say the actual number is 240,000.

November 8

President Bush announces an increase in US forces in the gulf region, which will result in the deployment of 200,000 more troops.

About the Author

Robert F. Dorr is a writer, lecturer and photographer specializing in modern military issues. Dorr served in the US Air Force in Korea 1957-60, and studied the Korean language at the Monterey (California) Institute of Foreign Studies. As a career foreign service officer with the Department of State, he was posted as a diplomat in Tananarive, Seoul, Fukuoka, Monrovia, Stockholm and London. Now retired, Dorr lives in Oakton, Virginia, with his wife Young Soon and his two sons, Bobby and Jerry. Dorr's previous books include: *Vietnam Combat from the Cockpit, Vietnam MiG Killers, Big Bombers: Strategic Air Command's B-52s, Swingwings, and Stealth,* and, with photographer Robert Ketchell, *Wings of Gold: Earning Your US Navy Wings.*

Now from Motorbooks International, THE POWER SERIES provides an in-depth look at the troops, weapon systems, ships, planes, machinery and missions of the world's modern military forces. From training to battle action, the top military units are detailed and illustrated with top quality color and black and white photography.

Available through book shops and specialty stores or direct. Call toll free 1–800–826–6600. From overseas 1–715–294–3345 or fax 1–715–294–4448

AIRBORNE: Assault from the Sky—
by Hans Halberstadt
America's front line parachute divisions

AIR GUARD: America's Flying Militia—
by George Hall
From the cockpit on their flying missions

ARMY AVIATION—by Hans Halberstadt
American power house; how it evolved, how it works

C-130: The Hercules—by M. E. Morris
Full technical and operations analysis on this sky truck

CV: Carrier Aviation—
by Peter Garrison and George Hall
Directly from the flight deck

GREEN BERETS: Unconventional Warriors—by Hans Halberstadt
"To liberate from oppression"

ISRAEL'S ARMY—by Samuel M. Katz
Inside this elite modern fighting force

MARINE AIR: First to Fight—
by John Trotti and George Hall
America's most versatile assault force

NTC: A Primer of Modern Mechanized Combat—by Hans Halberstadt
The US National (Tank and Helicopter) Training Center

SAC: A Primer of Modern Strategic Airpower—by Bill Yenne
American bomber force analyzed

STRIKE: US Naval Strike Warfare Center—
by John Joss and George Hall
US Navy's "Top Gun" for ground attack pilots

TOP GUN: The Navy's Fighter Weapons School—by George Hall
The best of the best

USAFE: A Primer of Modern Air Combat in Europe—by Michael Skinner and George Hall
Ever alert in an ever-changing world

USAREUR: The United States Army in Europe—by Michael Skinner
Sister title to USAFE

USCG: Always Ready—by Hans Halberstadt
Coast Guard search and rescue, Alaska patrol and more

USN: Naval Operations in the '80s—
by Michael Skinner
In-depth analysis of today's American Navy

SPACE SHUTTLE: The Quest Continues—
by George J. Torres
Pre-shuttle and shuttle operations history

More titles are constantly in preparation